I GAVE AWAY ALL MY CLOTHES

I Gave Away All My Clothes

LIVING OUT VALUES THROUGH SOCIAL ENTREPRENEURSHIP

Andy Lower
Andy Showell-Rogers

Contents

In memoriam

In memory of the lives lost at Rana Plaza and in honour of the millions of garment workers around the world who labour in oppressive conditions.

Before

24th April 2013 - The Rana Plaza Disaster

The Rana Plaza building was located twenty miles outside the Bangladeshi capital of Dhaka, in a suburb called Savar. It was a four-storey building that started life in 2006 to house shops and banks. Over the next few years, clothing factories gradually moved in, despite warnings that the building was not structured to cope with the weight and vibrations of the heavy machinery that they needed to function. Between 2008 and 2012, the building's owner gave his permission for four additional storeys to be built on top of the original four levels, in direct violation of local building code regulations but justified to meet the massive demand for cheap, exportable clothes.

At the time of the building's collapse, six different clothing factories operated within the building. A ninth storey was being constructed in early 2013 in order to increase production of more cheap clothes. The workers there were making clothes for Matalan, Primark, Wal-Mart, Benetton, and other Western fast fashion brands.

On Tuesday, 23rd April 2013, large cracks appeared in the side of the building and an inspection engineer urged the immediate evacuation of the premises. Despite the warnings, factory workers were told to return to work later that same day. Deadlines needed to be met. Western brands needed their cheap clothes. Consumers had money to be spent. Workers were reminded that if they did not return to their stations, they would not be paid and would immediately lose their jobs and thereby their income, for their families. They were assured that the building was safe. It was a lie.

At 8:45 the next morning there was a power cut. When the generators on the top of the building kicked in to restore power, the sudden shudder from their vibrations was the final straw. The building structure gave way and completely collapsed. Over 2,500 people were inside the building at the time. Almost half of them died.

Overview

"What do you think about when you're buying clothes? Do you like it? Can you afford it? Does it fit?

What about who made it? Or were they treated fairly?

Last year 1,129 people died when the Rana Plaza Building factory in Bangladesh collapsed. We were confronted with who made our clothes and the conditions that they worked in."

These were the opening lines of our crowdfunding campaign to launch Visible Clothing in April 2014 (tragically the number of these individual lives lost would later increase to 1,134). A decade later, these are the same questions that we ask ourselves whenever we are in a conversation about clothing.

If you had told either of us when we first met over 20 years ago that we would be writing a book about our role in the clothing sector, we would have laughed and laughed. We still do! We are not, and never will be, fashionistas. At best we pride ourselves on being and looking normalish (or at least trying to!). However, over the last decade of our journey in the ethical clothing space, we have learned so much about the psychology of fashion, and specifically, the unique and critical role that clothing has. It is one of the principal outward expressions of our identity. How we dress demonstrates who we are and, both actively and passively, says a lot about us as individuals.

Over the years we have heard so many people make the legendary statement, "You guys should write a book". While we dabbled with the idea and looked to find ways to share our story, it was the COVID pandemic and its horrific impact on the ethical clothing sector, and specifically on our business, that provided both the time and the urgency to write things down. Our vision has always been to make the connection between consumers and workers more direct and visible than ever. Our wild ride running Visible brought these two worlds closely together and we hope this book does that for you as the reader.

As we were writing this book, we reflected on the huge number of lessons that we have learned and the experiences that we have been fortunate to have. The good. The bad. And the ugly. While this book shares our story, it is by no means a blueprint or a 'must-do' guide to follow. It's meant to encourage you, the reader, to see more clearly the reality of the world we live in and to be aware of the profound difference you, the consumer, can make through ethical clothing purchases. While we do not expect everyone to suddenly give away all their clothes like we did (although that would be a fascinating social experiment!), we do hope to challenge you to embark further on your own personal journey as an ethical consumer, shopping in line with values. Throughout this book, we try to be vulnerable, honest, and visible about our own journey. Writing this book took a lot of soul searching. While helpful and therapeutic, it was also challenging and painful. As we unpack the background of the current dark world of modern day fast-fashion, we hope that you'll share some of the roller coaster experience with us.

This book is separated into two sections that are focused on our two primary goals. Firstly, we want to help dispel the most common reasons that consumers give for why they can't shop in line with their values. As we share some personal stories about our initial journey in ethical clothing, we hope to bring awareness to the impact that our individual purchasing directly has on others. Whether we accept responsibility or not, we believe that customers have massive power and that where money is spent has an impact that is either positive or negative. What we buy speaks loudly about what we really value and who we truly are: the actions that we take reflect who we are and we all know that actions speak louder than words.

Secondly, this book shares a story about social entrepreneurship. Our story. The real story. We hope that by sharing glimpses into the successes and failures that we experienced along the way, we will be able to both challenge and encourage you on the journey of values alignment. By sharing the reality of social entrepreneurship, we hope that you too will come away with a feeling of hope, of optimism. We hope you will laugh with us at our comedic mistakes; cry with us at the injustices in our world; and most importantly, feel both inspired and hopeful about the huge opportunity for positive social change. You can make a difference in the world simply by intentionally choosing to buy clothes in line with your values.

We can live in denial of the truth, or turn a blind eye to it as much as we'd like, but the facts remain the same: buying clothes in the mainstream clothing sector directly impacts and perpetuates the trap of extreme poverty. Millions of people, typically without formal education or financial options, are left with minimal opportunities and life choices. It's not right and we, as a society, have to make a change. We hope that by reading this book you will be inspired AND think through what change-making action might look like for you personally.

We are Andy Lower and Andy Showell-Rogers. Andy Lower is a qualified barrister with a background in international development and impact investing. Andy Showell-Rogers has a diverse background in international human resources and leveraging technology for business sustainability. We are both strong believers in market-forces and believe that business can be a critical component to bring about lasting change. Additionally, we are also socially-minded citizens, mindful of the reality that we are part of a much larger ecosystem; interconnected in such a way that we can have ripple effects well beyond what we can personally see or directly experience.

We're both Brits, so this has been written and edited in British English as opposed to American or Australian English. Learned as opposed to learnt; recognise as opposed to recognize etc etc. Hopefully we've removed all the major faux paux (that's as much French as we'll include!), but be prepared for some Britishisms as you read!

This book does not intend to guilt or shame anyone, but instead to provoke thought and to provide suggestions for positive, practical steps. We have a positive outlook on the opportunities in ethical clothing. However, we have intentionally tried to share honestly, and as you'll read there were many challenges and complexities that we as a values-driven business experienced along the way. We'd love for the world to be as black and white as we once imagined it to be, but the reality is that there is a lot of grey. Through this journey, we have seen time and time again the need to embrace this ambiguity in order to bring about lasting change. To sit with the discomfort that is reality. Holding on to the values that are black and white, while trying to be morally wise with the areas that have more grey, allows for greater progress towards one's mission.

A few points to note: This book shares data and quotes reports that for ease of readership are listed in the appendix at the end. Many of these reports were read at the start of our journey in 2013 and so while still very relevant, are now over a decade old. We have added in some updated reports, as so many of these issues remain the same many years later. Rather than interrupting the flow of the writing, we've tried to ensure that we've acknowledged the source of the information and then included a full list at the end of the book. We'd love to have shared more details but tried to accurately summarise incredible research in a digestible format.

Similarly, each chapter heading is somewhat long as it tries to sum up what the chapter is about. Each chapter could be a book in and of itself. We are aware that we just touched on the surface on many of these topics and didn't have the space to do full justice to these important themes.

The stories of both of us have been very intertwined on this journey and so we have blurred and blended the stories in this book. In order to keep things simple we have the voice of both of us presented by a singular 'Andy'. We are thankful for those who have shared their experiences with us and we have tried to be honest, respectful and visible in sharing their personal stories. As we highlight specific stories about colleagues and others who we worked, we have intentionally changed many of the names to respect their confidentiality and tried to respect their personal privacy by not sharing personal details that are not ours to share. We aimed to reflect as honestly and accurately as we can, sharing our personal highs and lows, acutely aware of the benefit of hindsight and how perceptions can change when there is a chance for reflection. We are also aware of how much we still have to learn about the ethical clothing sector and look forward to learning more!

There are many people that we need to thank, who we acknowledge with thanks and appreciation at the end of the book. But critically at the start, we must thank both of our wives. It was our individual choice to go all in on this journey and yet too often Caroline and Jessica have been the ones that had to experience the consequences of our choices! They've listened to us, challenged us, supported us, and we're so thankful for them encouraging us to be the best of us.

Additionally, there is one more person we wanted to thank right at the beginning. There were three of us on our initial journey into ethical clothing. We will forever be indebted to John 'Johnald' Payne, not only for being the genius that came up with the name 'Visible' but for playing such an integral role in the first part of our journey. Johnald tragically suddenly passed away on September 29th 2016. We are thankful for his incredible role in our lives; and for the love and compassion he showed to the most marginalised in our world, including workers in the apparel industry whom he had never met. We reference Johnald specifically at various points in the book, but his impact was more profound than those occasional shout-outs.

It has indeed been a wild ride. It's hard to overstate just how much learning there is to be had from operating a social enterprise. On this adventure, we have had to frequently pivot and adjust. The daily challenges of trying to be a values-driven business provide incredible highs and devastating lows, forcing a lot of self-reflection. It's been a journey of consistent learning, often through struggles. Yet, we remain convinced that buying in line with our ethical values can change the world. We have seen it; we have lived it; and we want to share it with you in the hope that you'll continue to access your role in it. This is our story. The story of Visible Clothing.

To a world where everyone in the clothing sector is treated fairly!

Cheers,

Andy & Andy
April 2024

PART I - The Four 'Buts' of Ethical Clothing

1

Starting on our journey: Giving away all our clothes

October 2013

I'll never forget when Andy and I had 'the call'. With one of us having just lost our job and the other recovering from some challenging health issues, we were both in seasons of life that provided us with the opportunity to re-evaluate and reassess. We were open to finding and committing to our next chapter, whatever that was going to be. We had been wanting to spend more time together and so rather than just syncing up our TV watching list or signing up for a fantasy football league (like normal people do), our conversation drifted before we ended up focusing on ethical clothing.

We had both been passionate about issues connected to global poverty for as long as we could remember and had been involved in social justice work professionally for years, leading various initiatives and speaking at a variety of conferences. Like many others, we were committed to talking about the right thing. We were very committed... to talking. We'd happily sign the petition when someone asked us to, or give money away to various causes and groups. We'd even shake our heads and wave our fists at the TV screen every once in a while. But, while we knew in our hearts that we personally could do more, it just seemed so hard to take things to the next level. It always felt like there were barriers that stopped us from moving forward, obstacles that stopped us from not just talking a good game, but actually moving to changing our lifestyles.

We were both fortunate enough to have travelled and to have met and connected with people who - from a monetary perspective - were far less fortunate than ourselves. We'd also studied and read up on historical injustices and the devastating impact that global inequality had on the most marginalised in our world. And yet, the 'buts' held us back from ever doing more.

On that call, for the very first time, we discussed the Rana Plaza disaster in Bangladesh, and how it had distressed us both. Its profound impact wasn't lost on us, however quickly it had vanished from our TV screens and been removed from our immediate focus. While the impact was devastating, it was buried deep below the immediacy and urgency of everyday life. Over the next month after our initial 'call', our conversations took twists and turns, as we tried to unpack the excuses as to why it was so hard to buy ethical clothes.

To be honest, many of the excuses had some basis in reality. We had periodically tried to buy ethical clothing in the past, but the quality or the look just wasn't there for what we needed. Even when we set out to get something specifically in the fair-trade section of the shop or website, intentionally limiting the options, we had to brace ourselves for the cost, which we knew would be substantially higher than we would ever be willing to pay if we were buying 'normal' clothes. At the end of the day, we weren't convinced that we were going to have any lasting impact, or that parting with our hard-earned pennies was actually going to make any long-term difference, so what was the point in even trying?

We talked about trying to make incremental changes and just how hard it all was. We kept coming back to the same four excuses, which we'll unpack in the first half of this book. We started to call them the '4 Buts':

1. But there isn't enough choice?
2. But it's too expensive?
3. But I want to look good?
4. But is there any real impact?

Gradually, we realised that these 'Buts' were the principal barriers stopping not only us, but other like-minded individuals from buying ethically made clothing. As we came to this realisation, we decided it was time to go big or go home.

We both agreed that the only way we would be able to commit to embracing ethical clothing was to go 'all in'. How about giving away all our clothes? No ifs, ands, or buts. No excuses. All in. Give away all our clothes and start again from scratch. Blank slate. And if we could hold each other accountable, then we had a much better chance of making it actually happen. It would be like having a workout partner who showed up at your doorstep every morning in their gym gear, forcing you to stick with the plan and get the workout done whether you wanted to or not. You didn't want to let your buddy down. And so, we focused on making it a simple two-part process: out with the old, in with the new.

We also decided it would be interesting to share the experience by writing a blog about it. Agreeing to regularly blog added the pressure of holding ourselves accountable to our wider network of friends and family. On the positive side, it had the potential to force us both to follow through on our commitment. On the negative side, it scarily increased the risk profile for us personally. It was one thing to look foolish in front of a buddy and our close family and there was always an option to back track if it didn't work out. It was a much bigger deal to look foolish in front of others outside of our immediate circle of trust. We'd first met each other at university and had done our fair share of fun and games as college students that no doubt showed our immature and foolish ways (thankfully in the world before smartphones!), but now we were supposed to be trustworthy and mature adults. We weren't yet old enough for a mid-life crisis, but we were very aware that we weren't as young as we used to be. What kind of full-grown adult gives away ALL their clothes?

As we prepared to give our entire wardrobes away, our nervousness increased. Whether we were able to find clothes to meet our ethical commitment was still the big unknown question. But, as of January 1st, 2014, ready or not, we would no longer have any of our old clothes. We had to make it work because every single item of clothing we owned - socks, undergarments, the lot - would be gone. Both of us had 'normal' extensive wardrobes with 'normalish' clothes (well, mine more than his!) but for both of us, buying an entirely new wardrobe made up of 100% ethically produced items was going to be a significant undertaking.

We both knew that we had to have a serious values realignment so that our purchases would match the values that we claimed to have. We were ready, sort of. We were excited, nervously. But, we were focused and committed to our goal. We were going to go for it: give away all our clothes and start over. We knew what we had seen in the clothing sector wasn't right and wanted to get a lot more educated, so we decided to do some serious research into the murky world of clothing manufacturing. We had no idea what we were about to discover as we lifted up that rock to see what was underneath. This wasn't just theory, this was real. It impacted individual lives.

Stark Injustices for Workers in the Clothing Industry

When we talked about the Rana Plaza disaster and the plight of the garment workers, we often wondered what was going through the workers' minds as they went to work on that fateful day, Wednesday, 24th April 2013. The workers knew that the building wasn't safe. They could see the cracks in the wall. They had even complained to management about the working conditions. Yet still, they went to work. Why? Why did they make a choice that looks so crazy from our perspective? Why in the world would any person willingly go into a building to work under conditions that were clearly so dangerous?

As we reflected on this question, we applied our logic to this situation. If it was one of us who was born in Bangladesh instead of being born in the UK, and who worked in a clothing factory, we wouldn't have gone to work that morning in a building that looked like it was going to collapse at any minute. Surely? We would have undertaken a risk/reward analysis. Consciously or subconsciously, we are evaluating risk options every day, often quickly and without great reflection. However, when it comes to something important or potentially life-changing, we slow down to look at the options in more detail. We take risks, but not ridiculous ones where the odds are not in our favour. We're not foolish. But neither were the hundreds of Bangladeshi garment workers. So why did they go in?

While the Rana Plaza workers might not have had the same academic backgrounds as we did, they had their own personal experiences and a wealth of generational wisdom to rely on to make good, wise, common sense choices. And if they had the choice; surely wisdom and common sense would have guided them not to go to work in an unsafe building.

IF. If they had a choice. The more we've learned about the Rana Plaza factory workers and the plight of the average garment labourer, the more we've come to understand the terrible trap that they faced. Most garment workers live within the soul-destroying, life-defining reality of being born into extreme poverty. From the day they are born, they are caught in the extreme poverty trap.

In Bangladesh alone there are over 3.5 million people working in garment factories. Add in the numbers from other countries across Asia (where 75% of the world's garment workers come from, and where many working conditions can be equally as bad as those at Rana Plaza) and you're looking at millions of people. Tens of millions of people. And that number multiplies significantly when including family members who cannot work, the old, the very young, but who are reliant on the income of garment workers.

Most of these workers are women, and many are children. In the vast majority of cases, they are paid unfair wages. They consistently work unreasonably long hours with no overtime pay. They labour for hours without adequate breaks. The buildings in which they toil and sweat often pose grave safety hazards. The oppressive conditions are legion, and hard for us to even comprehend. Labourers often lack the power to speak out against it.

We'll unpack more of the challenges that are experienced by garment workers later in this book, but perhaps the biggest eye opener from our initial research was how consistently hard garment labourers work, and how unfair it all is. Regardless of how hard they work, it's almost impossible for them to improve their situation. With low and late pay, many factory workers attempt to earn a living wage by working overtime. And yet, even with all those extra hours worked, it is almost impossible to get out of the poverty trap. A couple of examples made this painfully clear to us as we reviewed some 'Labour Behind The Label' reports from 2012:

- In Sri Lanka, surveys showed that, in order to meet basic needs, a worker must earn US $320 a month. The minimum wage for workers there is just US $80 per month. Workers therefore scramble to get extra hours of work in the hopes of being able to bridge that insurmountable gap.
- In Cambodia, long-hours are a particular scourge of the sweat-shop industry. Independent third-party reports show that most workers are working between three and five hours of overtime per day. That's eleven to thirteen-hour days in hot factories to make clothes for Westerners to wear on a warm,

casual, summer evening out. In 95% of the factories that were surveyed, overtime was not an exception, but the rule.

○ Working long hours puts workers' long-term health at serious risk, as evidenced by the fainting outbreaks that became commonplace in Cambodia's garment factories. One example came from the Huey Chuen factory producing for Western high-street brands that had thirty workers in the same stitching section experience an incident of mass fainting in 2012. The workers described the factory as being exceptionally hot, with heat-generating machines working non-stop in cramped conditions. Several people complained of respiratory trouble, before the workers began to faint en masse. Workers told Labour Behind the Label that if an employee refused to work overtime on three occasions, she would be fired. The same workers also reported at least one fainting incident every day in the factory.

"They faint when they have overtime work for about three and a half hours per day. It is because they are too tired, they don't have enough food or they don't have good quality food".

2

Our reflections on ourselves: The true value of clothes

As I prepared to give all the clothes away, I took them out of my wardrobe and dumped them on my bed. The first thing that struck me was the sheer volume of clothes. The stack was massive. Somehow my 'normal' wardrobe seemed to have expanded during its journey off the hangers and out of the drawers. It had ballooned in size! How, I wondered, did I ever think that I needed this many clothes? Just lugging all these clothes around was exhausting. It made me slightly dizzy. It almost made me feel like fainting. Ugh. The sickening irony.

The True Value Of Clothes

Out of sheer curiosity, I began pulling items from the mountain of garments on my bed and counting them. There were 35 t-shirts, 7 sweaters/jumpers, 6 pairs of smartish-casual trousers, 2 pairs of jeans, 6 wearable suits, 18 pairs of boxers (that's almost three weeks' worth without washing!), 6 pairs of shorts and 51 shirts. To be precise, there were 41 shirts in good enough condition to be given away to someone else and 10 that were definitely not good enough to be given away but were good enough for me to justify wearing when I needed them (even if they were almost threadbare!).

41 shirts? How on earth could I have had more than three-dozen shirts? That's more than one shirt a day for a whole month. And, with 41 shirts at my disposal, how could I never seem to be able to find the right one, or a clean one to wear?! Until I'd made the decision to give it all away, it had never struck me before how much choice I had in what I wore each day.

As I looked into the hollow space in my wardrobe which my clothes used to fill, I felt a sense of trepidation. I imagine feeling like my kids did when their favourite comforter was taken away, or how Linus from Charlie Brown would feel without his blankie. How was I going to manage without all this stuff? Not only were there memories attached to various outfits (especially the threadbare ones) but there was also some sort of reassurance in the volume of clothes that surrounded me. I couldn't remember all the details, but there must have been a reason why I had acquired each of these items... And yet, in the mix of all the emotions, the thought of being free of these clothes was incredibly liberating. The thought of being able to be rid of all the stuff was a breath of fresh air. Stuff, stuff, stuff. I had waaaaay too much stuff. Since Andy and I had committed to do this together, and to share it with our networks, I knew that I couldn't reverse the decision, so I decided to fully embrace the feeling of freedom from stuff.

Where to Give our Clothes Away

Given the moral basis behind the gutting of our wardrobes, we agreed to be as intentional as possible as to how we dispensed with our old clothes. Unexpectedly, the giving away of our clothes turned out to be one of the biggest highlights of this whole process. Not only did it provide us with a great education on the personal connection between emotions and clothes, but there were a lot of unexpected joys as the true value of clothes, both those that I cared about deeply, as well as those that we'd undervalued, became apparent.

I was astonished by how many clothes in my wardrobe were simply unwearable. Why did I feel the need to keep those additional ten shirts with all their holes and loose threads? While they had been wearable to me for years and I had learned to fold the cuffs in a certain way to hide the fact that they were threadbare or to wear the comfy t-shirt always with a sweatshirt to hide the nasty ketchup stain that wouldn't go away, in all honesty, a lot of these clothes should have been cast out years ago. They were not really wearable to me, and I certainly could not imagine them being wearable to anyone else.

While owning a lot of clothes, as encouraged by the prevailing fast fashion culture, we weren't really into fast fashion. By that, I mean to say that it wasn't in our mindset to just buy an outfit with the intention to just wear it once or twice. We weren't following the latest trends and were far from shopping addicts. We kept clothes for years, which is one of the reasons that we had so many.

We looked for different ways to repurpose items that couldn't be reworn, but aside from the hoodie with holes in it that the dog appreciated as additional bedding in his kennel, and the handful of t-shirts that could be used as rags for work in the garage, a good third of the wardrobe had reached its end of life. So, it was dumped in the bin to be taken to the landfill. Seeing this happen in one large dump was humbling, and much more distressing than periodic smaller dumps. Fabrics all have an end of life, but surely there has to be a better way than to simply dump our castoffs in a landfill for the next generations to deal with? I was made painfully aware of my contribution to the estimated 350,000 tonnes of clothes dumped in landfills annually in the UK alone. In hindsight, we could have done more to be zero-waste, but that wasn't our primary focus at this stage. We didn't research the complications and opportunities with zero-waste until much later on our journey. So, off to the landfill went a third of my clothes.

When I cleaned up my sock drawer I was amazed to learn just how many odd socks I had! Odd because the washing machine monster seemed to have eaten a number of them over the years, but also odd because of the large number of holey ones that I had convinced myself I could still keep wearing even if my big toe was sticking out. My brother-in-law was only too happy to take the wearable odd socks off my hands to add to his odd sock drawer. Apparently, that's what the cool kids now use every day!

Emptying the whole wardrobe meant that bags upon bags of clothes were piled up to be donated to various groups that were willing to have them. We each ended up giving the majority of our clothes to various social groups or non-profits. The clear highlight of this process was working with the 'Dress For Success' program at a nearby prison. When I rang the program director to ask if they could do anything with six lightly worn suits, I was inspired by his level of enthusiasm. He ran a program that was designed to collect unwanted, but still wearable clothes, to give to former inmates to wear as they stepped out of jail and returned to society. As they met their loved ones again for the first time in months or years, they were able to walk out in a nice suit. His program focused on just how critical this first impression was for those leaving jail to meet with their families, and how powerful clothing could be as part of the rehabilitation process. In addition to a good first impression, the suits could be worn at the job centre and for job interviews as people began the process of rebuilding their lives.

As I learned more about the program, the program director's initial somewhat personal questions - "how old are you?" and "what size were you when you wore these suits?" - made more and more sense. Typically, the suits that he received were those from family members who were cleaning out the wardrobe of an older deceased man, or from men who had gone on a weight reduction plan and wanted to get rid of the clothes that they hoped never to fit into again. This was the first time that he had received any 'normal' suits - meaning suits that would fit an average sized man, that were semi-fashionable and that would give a great first impression for those stepping outside.

Wow! The thought hit me; beyond finding somewhere to simply dump a bunch of unwanted clothes, this donation could truly have a positive impact on people's lives. It was perhaps the clearest example of just how much value clothes have; more than simply just monetary value in what was spent to buy them, but value in terms of what clothes mean to us as individuals; what story clothes tell others about us; and how clothes help to define our place in society.

Our Criteria for Buying New Clothes

Faced with the prospect of re-stocking our freshly emptied wardrobes with only ethically made clothes, we agreed to set up some objective criteria about where we would buy new clothes. We chose not to buy second-hand clothes from charity shops or thrift stores. We generally support the positive social impact of reusing and recycling clothes, and understand that buying in charity shops or thrift stores helps to avoid negative impacts for garment workers and generates income for charities. However, so much donated clothing actually ends up in landfills, and we'd seen first-hand how much the charity shop model can undercut job creation in emerging economies where unwanted clothes are sent and then resold.

We didn't simply want to just withdraw our support of the abusive manufacturers in the garment industry in order not have a negative impact in the sector. Instead, we wanted to take that support, and channel it to clothing manufacturers in emerging economies who were already doing good and having a positive impact. In other words, avoiding being part of the problem wasn't enough. We aimed to proactively find ways to become part of the solution.

In the past, we had bought most of our clothes brand new, and so changing that habit and buying used clothing would rob us of an opportunity to find and support companies that were having a positive impact on the world. We wanted our money to go to those brands and suppliers who were working hard to redeem the clothing sector; to support companies that provided their workers with fair wages and safe working conditions. We knew that there were good factory owners and businesses out there, mostly under the radar of mainstream consumers. These companies were driven by a motivation to change the world and placed people as a priority in their business practices. We were committed to invest in them, even if it was just a relatively tiny amount of cash, through the clothes that we bought from them. It needed to be more than a guilt offering. We were aiming to create in ourselves a whole new way of thinking and a whole different approach to shopping.

Over several weeks we went back and forth, trying to find objective standards for creating a wardrobe of what we considered to be fairly made clothes. We ended up with five criteria that we felt were appropriate for our mission:

#1 Ethically Sourced – a DNA of Fairness

First, we wanted to make sure that the clothes we were buying were not just simply made by fairly paid workers, but were also ethically produced. These might seem like trifling semantics, but for us this was an important distinction. From our perspective, ethical meant that the clothing company worked with vendors who treated workers well, respected local culture, had humane business policies, and used raw materials that were environmentally sustainable. We committed to find businesses that were established to do things fundamentally differently to the current status quo.

Our goal was to only own clothes made by workers who were both paid fairly, and produced by manufacturers who treated their supply chain partners ethically. Ethical production involves an awareness of the impacts of sourcing decisions all the way down the line. Values were the key and the workers throughout the supply chain needed to be treated with values that aligned with ours.

Initially, this meant that we were focused only on companies and organisations that had some sort of fair-trade certification or third-party validation. While this was a great starting point and as we looked into the sector further, we realised that the certification world was itself incredibly complicated and had multiple variations on who was certifying who, along with what exactly was being certified. Additionally, when we questioned and researched brands, there were a number that were not certified, often because they were too small to be able to justify the cost of certification, even though they had a clear commitment to fairness and were, in our opinion, some of the most ethical companies that we found.

As we researched how to rebuild our wardrobes, we spent a lot of time trying to set up objective ways to assess the 'DNA' of companies and brands that we were buying from. We began to recognize patterns that reflected a company's commitment to ethics. It was not easy, and we could spend hours being hypercritical asking more and more questions. Each company had human founders and no-one was perfect. It was impossible to do everything perfectly. We couldn't even agree amongst ourselves what was right in many situations! However, we started to see patterns that were reflective of what a company or brand really stood for. It was all about their DNA, and at the core, it was all about their overriding commitment to fairness and values.

#2 Environmentally Sustainable

While we had initially started on this journey motivated by the human catastrophe that took place at Rana Plaza, it doesn't take a rocket scientist to realise the potentially irreversible impact that our clothing purchases are having on the planet. As we went deeper into our ethical clothing journey, it was alarming to learn just how devastating the clothing sector has been on the environment. This is a catastrophe that is going to be felt long into the future.

The Rana Plaza disaster had a devastating, immediate and direct impact on thousands of lives, but when it comes to the longer-term environmental impact of plundering from the earth and polluting the skies, the clothing sector has been a leader across the board. From the sourcing of the materials and the prevalence of single-use plastics; to the production and creation of synthetic fabrics; to the massive amount of discarded waste across the whole process. It goes all the way from the start through to the end of the life of a garment. The environmental damage from clothing is disastrous. Truly unfathomable.

We committed to finding and buying products that were made of organic materials wherever possible, but were aware that our control of this criteria was sometimes limited due to the challenges of many products not being 100% organic. Therefore, we focused on damage limitation whenever we could, while learning more about the complexity of this issue. In addition to having a preference for organics, we were also looking for companies that were proactive in changing societal norms: companies that demonstrated a desire to think about waste management differently: use of renewables, pioneering fabrics, a focus on regenerative agriculture, and an over-all clear intention to having a positive environmental impact.

#3 Internationally Made

We committed to only buying clothes that had been made in emerging economies. There are some fantastic ethical clothing companies sourcing and producing in the UK and the USA (where we were both living) that pay their workers well, treat them fairly, and are conscientious about using ethically sourced materials. However, buying from Western markets didn't align with our specific goals. Most of the world's clothing is produced in emerging markets. As we assessed the clothes that we were giving away, we were shocked to learn that roughly 95% of our old wardrobes had been manufactured in emerging economies. We didn't want to avoid the reality of international clothing production and decided that if we were to buy our new wardrobes from companies that had been produced in a totally different marketplace with Western government regulations, we would again be avoiding the problem rather than working towards a solution. If the economy of a country like Bangladesh is dependent on the clothes that their citizens make, was it the most impactful to simply boycott the clothes manufactured there?

We chose instead to be proactive in finding companies and brands that were using alternative models in those same countries. We determined that supporting ethical clothing sectors in countries with higher GDP (aka wealthier countries) was not going to improve conditions for the people we were hoping to impact. Instead, we wanted to focus on redeeming and improving industry practices in the places with the greatest need for reform. We committed to only buy from brands that had already made a commitment to treating garment workers fairly internationally.

#4 Directly Impacting Extreme Poverty

Not only did we want to buy from companies working in emerging markets, but we also wanted to have a direct and positive impact on extreme poverty. We felt that we could have a bigger impact on the world if we allocated our money to buying clothes from companies who were supporting workers to break free from the trap of extreme poverty. The causes of extreme poverty are complex, and in countries without structured financial safety nets, it is easier for people to slip into dire circumstances and is harder for them to escape out of the cycle of extreme poverty. Missing a day's work because of illness, getting paid late, or having a baby, can easily thwart a family who have been working their way out of extreme poverty, and force them back into the poverty cycle. Because those most marginalised in society are the demographic that produce most of the clothes that Western consumers purchase, we wanted to try to find companies and brands that were working effectively with that demographic.

#5 Positive 'Theory of Change'

Lastly, we looked to buy from companies that were not just working with those trapped in extreme poverty, but who were proactively trying, beyond paying them fairly, to have a positive impact in the lives of their workforce. It was our belief that buying our new wardrobes from factories that treated their workers well would help stimulate a cascade of positive knock-on impacts. While we disagree with the nonsensical view of 'trickle down economics' that only truly impacts the most wealthy, stable income from work for the most marginalised provides truly positive ripple-effects. For example, if women employees with maternity leave rights are freed from the fear that a pregnancy would cost them their job there are clear positive ripple effects for children. If parents employed in local factories can be saved from lengthy commutes to find work in other urban locations, they are freed to spend more time at home with their families. In emerging markets too many children are frequently forced to grow up far too fast. Those born into families that don't have the basic necessities are often forced to work in the home and raise younger siblings. In our eyes, pro-actively buying from companies where there was values alignment was critical.

We felt strongly that our decision to buy only from brands that met these criteria would give us a template for making a more profound impact. We were looking to find brands that explicitly shared what they were doing to fulfil their moral obligation to their workforce. Criteria are great in theory; but their real value increases exponentially when they are applied first-hand and directly to those actually working on the ground. In order to fully understand, it is critical to remember those who were working on the ground and their reality. Listening with an open mind was the name of the game, as we learnt time and time again.

3

Going to Rana Plaza, Bangladesh: Learning firsthand

April 14th, 2014.

"Look over there. There's a way to get in."

I hadn't spotted it, but my generous host, Saif, who I had met just a few hours earlier was now pulling corrugated iron sheets aside to make the hole in the fence wider. I had asked for a closer look, and that was exactly what I was going to get. We joined local workers in exploiting a gap in the fence that had been pried open to create a shortcut path. This was the main entry for some of the hundreds of labourers who sewed at this factory. It was one of the multitude of production facilities in the neighbourhood.

Once inside, I started to appreciate how flat the ground was in comparison to the multi-storey buildings that loomed above us. We were standing in a gap in a long line of giant dominos. I followed Saif, a local labour rights campaigner, and we stumbled through the leftover debris. There were no walls left to protect us from the sun, which was always going to be a struggle for me; a pasty white Englishman in the scorching Bangladeshi heat. As we reached our destination, the endless noise of the city disappeared into the thick, misty air. For what felt like an eternity, we simply stood in silence. This site that used to house one of the city's busiest clothing factories was reduced to ruins. As the sun scorched the rubble, I paused to take it all in. Here I was, standing in Rana Plaza.

Rana Plaza, Bangladesh, was where 1,134 men, women and children died because they did what hundreds of millions of people do every day without so much as a second thought; they went to work. However, different from what hundreds of millions of others do, they went to work in a ticking time bomb of a building who's time was up, that was not safe, and that should have been shut down. They had left their homes that morning, and every workday previously, to try to provide financially for their families. They went to work to make clothes, clothes for people like you and me.

This was reality.

I felt physically sick.

I'd seen the passing screenshot on the nightly news coverage of the Rana Plaza disaster and had spent hours following up and reading all about the tragedy; I'd read about the building that wasn't fit for any purpose but that continued to function as a factory; I'd been shocked to learn about its owners doubling the height of the building; about them adding storey on top of storey so that clothing companies could cram in more workers to make more clothes to make more money by selling those clothes to the eager Western buyers. It was disgusting. Yet, the real tragic reality was that this wasn't abnormal in the 21st century. These were status quo practices in the mainstream clothing sector. This was 'normal'. This had been allowed to happen.

I'd heard the horrific stories of the brutal deaths of 1,134 Bangladeshis and the grisly tales of those who survived. My stomach had turned as I'd reflected on how trapped survivors drank the blood of the dead as they fought to stay alive for days on end. I'd been able to digest the horrid details reflectively better over print media that had more detail than just the initial glimpse of it flashing across my TV screen. So, I thought I couldn't be shocked further. I thought that I was going to be primed for what I was about to see: rubble and remote grief. Heartbreakingly, nothing could have prepared me for what it felt like to stand on the site of this century's worst industrial disaster, knowing that under my feet, almost literally, lay unrecovered bodies. Lives that had been ended all too soon.

Standing where the Rana Plaza building used to be, I was overcome with guilt and shame. Guilt, because in a fractional way, I had played a part in causing this. Guilt, because I knew that my desire for cheap clothes had contributed to this senseless tragedy. Shame, because this should not have happened. Shame, because we as a society know better. Slowly, my guilt and shame turned to anger. Anger, because this did not need to have happened.

My anger grew as I reflected more on the reality of the world that we lived in. On that single day, Wednesday, 24th April, 2013, everything was forever changed for those 1,134 people and their surviving co-workers and families. Yet, in the wider clothing industry there was an initial outcry and then, as quick as a flash, it felt like nothing much changed, because the reality was that there was very little that did change. Many shoppers in the West barely noticed the Rana Plaza story as it was swallowed up immediately by the next news cycle. Most of the brands who were using the Rana

Plaza to make our clothes registered only a minor blip in sales, if they even noticed anything at all. On the ground in Bangladesh, garment workers continued to turn up for work, day-in and day-out in hazardous and unsafe environments. The socially acceptable oppressive clothing sector was allowed to carry on as if nothing had happened. It was shocking and, quite frankly, disgusting. How is this allowed to happen in our world today?

Having seen the photos of the collapsed factory on different news sites, and from different angles, I had come to view the site as a freeze-frame and hadn't really considered what lay outside the bounds of these photos. When I stood on the site and took in the view around the Rana Plaza, what struck me was that this was going on around the entire perimeter of its ruins. There was row upon row of factories full of garment workers. Each of them doing exactly what the workers of Rana Plaza had been doing that day – trying to make a living wage for their family. Working in horrific conditions that looked very similar to the ones that the workers entered into on that fateful morning of April 24th.

After an incredible day of learning more about the reality for workers in Rana Plaza style sweatshops, it was early evening and time to say goodbye to Saif. I made my way back to the hotel in a tuk-tuk. The streets were swarming with people as thousands of Bangladeshis came pouring out of factories to make their way home. The sheer volume of people surrounding us on every side made any rush-hour commute I'd ever experienced seem like a peaceful evening stroll. A handful were on their way home to spend time with their families, but I was reminded that for many, this was just a dinner break. They'd be returning to work after their meal to meet a deadline that their factory owners had ambitiously agreed to in order to keep a Western brand happy.

I was also told that despite the huge number of people that I could see walking around, there were many tens of thousands more who were still in the factories right now, some staying at work until after midnight. Fourteen-hour days, hazardous working conditions, and poor pay: this was the life of many Bangladeshi garment workers.

This was the life of the person who made my clothes and over 3 million more like them just in Bangladesh alone. This was what we as a society had chosen to buy into. This was the world of modern-day fast fashion.

Rana Plaza? Bangladesh? How had I got here? Lets step back in time 5 months to the 'great panic before Christmas' of 2013!

4

Less is more: But #1 - But there isn't enough choice?

One of the most exciting but also most stressful parts of Christmas shopping in 2013 was finding a way to overcome our biggest barrier - the lack of choice. Whenever we talked with friends who have looked into buying ethically made clothes, the primary complaint was that there wasn't enough choice. Looking at sales numbers, this is objectively correct. The size of the ethical clothing industry is miniscule compared to the mainstream clothing sector, and we as Western consumers have been conditioned to want a huge array of choices. Choice is a representation of the freedom that we value so much.

When I first started working with people in extreme poverty, I was told that the definition of poverty is: "the lack of choices". Those of us not living in poverty often think that we need loads of options to decide what we do or don't like. Not only do we want to have freedom to choose what we want, but often we are only able to make a buying decision when we are able to compare a potential purchase with other options. This was the biggest issue that left me disheartened when I first tried to buy ethical clothes. While not a regular casual scroller of clothing websites, and certainly never a leisure time window shopper, making decisions based on lots of choices and plenty of options was something that I, even as a casual Western consumer, had come to want and expect.

It was interesting to consider how we justify what we do with our purchasing power. Limited choice (which is statistically a fact) can often take the responsibility off of us as consumers. We understandably want to exercise our freedom of choice, so when options are narrowed down, we can very easily hide behind the excuse that 'we would do the right thing if only we could'. Our buying criteria for our new wardrobes was intentionally very narrow, and so we have further reduced our number of choices. While at the time, it required more effort than we sometimes wanted, even with our very narrow and specific criteria, the bottom line was that we managed to succeed. There was enough choice out there to buy in line with our values.

We each managed to succeed in our goal of upgrading our wardrobes and on reflection, the effort that we put in was relatively small. It wasn't a herculean task worthy of getting a medal. We were able to buy clothes from a wide variety of different brands and over time became repeat customers of a more select group of brands that we had come to appreciate. Even though clothes made ethically are indeed harder to find, the more time we spent looking, the more we were amazed at how many brands were out there. As the ethical sector has continued to grow and expand, many more brands exist today than when we started on this mission. And, as we got more and more into the process, we increasingly enjoyed the experience of evaluating the brands that were available. It was fascinating because lack of choice is the most popular 'But' that consumers, including us, use (or now used!), for not buying in line with values. Yet it was perhaps the most easily surmountable.

Lack of choice is far from an impossible barrier to overcome. Overcoming it gets a lot easier when we are prepared to turn the question of choice on its head and completely restructure the questions that we are asking ourselves when we make a purchase. What do you look for when you buy something to wear? Is it just about whether you like it, whether you can afford it, if it fits and is flattering? Or do you also care about who made it, whether they were treated fairly, or about how it was sourced? As we revised our questions, our starting point for how we made choices and what we wanted was fundamentally different. Our definition of 'choice' had substantially changed.

Less is More

Our wardrobes had shrunk dramatically since our journey began. Whereas before my clothes took up four drawers, three shelves, and one long hanger pole in the bedroom wardrobe, now they occupied a much smaller space: just one drawer, one shelf and five hangers. You read that right. Just five items of clothing hung in my closet.

But every day, I still had an incredible choice of things to wear. Even though it was considerably less than what we were able to do before. **I gained a whole new level of appreciation for what I had, rather than pining after what I didn't. We were able to do more with less.** When we actually took a good look into our 'before' wardrobes, we were left asking how many of these clothes did we actually wear? How many were 'throw-away clothes'—those cheap, fashionable, single-wear outfits that we bought in a fast fashion sale, buying quickly on sight rather than trying them on and thinking it through? How many clothes actually fit well? How many were of real quality? How many were we proud to wear as a reflection of our values and identity?

It's easy to see how short-sighted and unsustainable our choices are when we dump a single-use plastic container in the bin, or throw out heaps of packaging or filler from a delivery. Yet when it comes to clothing, we typically lack a long-term perspective. There isn't a prevalent belief in our culture that a consumer is investing in clothing products for the long-term. Fashion trends that are practically impossible to stay abreast of, as well as our regularly evolving body shapes (for better and worse!) can make it hard to have a long-term strategy for buying clothes. The need for short-term wins and immediate fixes as well as the desire to express creativity and personality, means that there is an understandable want to regularly refresh our wardrobes so that they can continue to be a reflection of who we are.

We found that by mixing and matching what we wore, we were able to make our new wardrobes, with a much smaller range of clothes, seem bigger. We had a different level of intentionality in what we chose to wear as we were left with only clothes that we actually liked. Less. Is. More! When we only own clothes that we love to wear and that we intentionally chose to invest in, we can adjust our expectations about how big a range of clothes we really need.

Increasing Our Choices Together

There's a vicious circle in the ethical clothing industry. Before consumers reframe their question of choice, they still focus on the fact that the range of clothes available is relatively limited, so the number of people committed to try to buy them is similarly limited. This has a direct impact on the companies trying to do genuine good in the world, as they don't get the money to increase the range of clothes they can offer and are left working with fewer resources. **The cycle repeats as a lack of choice leads to a continued lack of choice unless there is some substantial increase in investment to increase choice.**

This is the reason that so much of the Western world's online business goes to the handful of big players that are close to creating online monopolies. Visibility is driven by massive marketing budgets, consumption and reviews. Without those, products languish unseen in the shadow of all the other products, even if they are of superior quality. Positive consumer feedback offers reassurance to potential customers. We bring our repeat business to retailers that we know and trust. This makes the leap into the ethical clothing sector a daunting one for most shoppers, especially with brands that are not mainstream recognisable. However, each time we support an ethical company, we not only help ourselves in the purchase that we make, but we are collectively increasing the available choices and improving the market for the next like-minded customer.

As we became more educated ethical clothing consumers, we realised that our purchases actually made two positive important impacts. First, through our purchasing choices, we were able to support the human rights of garment workers in emerging markets. Second, our purchases supported the health of the businesses that sought to do good. By helping them in a small way to generate revenue, we were doing our part in ensuring the growth of their inventory and increased retail presence.

In the West, we are abundantly blessed with more choices than ever before. In many other parts of the world, workers are not so blessed. So perhaps the crux of the question is this: **will we limit our choices in order to increase the choices of others less fortunate than us?**

Will we choose to narrow our options when we go to buy a coat so a Colombian woman trapped in prostitution can find freedom by having a fairly paid job making quality clothing? Will we choose to limit our choice of T-shirts so the child of a factory worker in Uganda is more likely to go to high school? Will we limit our range of shoes so that an Ethiopian woman gets maternity leave to be with her newborn baby? All of those stories were real life impact stories that we were a part of. Being able to make a choice is a good thing, not just for those of us who are privileged by virtue of where we were born. It is incumbent upon us to use our freedom of choice for the good of others.

We are constantly making choices – knowingly or unknowingly. We make some choices with deep intentionality and we make other choices with flippant disregard for the consequences that can have massive impact on those around us. We might all have different views on how society should most effectively function, but at the core, empathy is one of the most, if not THE most, significant differentiators between humans and other animal species. The ability to look at life and situations from another's perspective is not only critical to a peaceful and orderly functioning society, but is imperative for sustainable success and economic growth. The collection of actionable choices that we make as individuals tells people around us who we really are, not grand intentions or words.

Three Men, Three Very Different Wardrobes

When we started on this journey, there were three of us that went all in. While we each claim to be 'normal-looking' and 'average-sized', each of us are quite different and this was reflected in the variation of items that we purchased. It would be a wild exaggeration to describe any of us as fashionable, but it is safe to say that despite our various styles each of us managed to get complete wardrobes that were a reflection of who we are. Being naturally competitive, we wanted to outdo each other and see who could come up with the 'best' wardrobe. We each came up with criteria that out-did the others - best price, best impact, best uniqueness (whatever that meant!) - but the winner was always the one who received the most compliments. After we'd rebooted our wardrobes, each of us found that we received more compliments on our clothing than we had ever before received. It was pleasantly surprising.

While our friends who knew what we were doing on this journey would relish any opportunity to mock us, frequently enquiring how regularly we had managed to change or wash our clothes, complete strangers consistently complimented us on our clothes. To be clear, we were still a long way from being fashionable and will never make it as models, but the fact that we were able to each find very different looking wardrobes with our limited selection criteria speaks to the fact that there is enough choice within the ethical clothing even for our specific tastes. While fashion faux pas were committed on a regular basis, especially by the other Andy, the 'compliments competition' helped keep us focused on the mission.

Bangladesh's Clothing Boom - The Cost of Choice

In the last twenty years, Bangladesh's clothing industry has exploded. As Western customers have demanded more options to choose from, fashion seasons have moved from the traditional two seasons, hot or cold, also known as spring/summer and autumn/winter, to a staggering new norm of fifty-two seasons a year. The impact for Bangladesh, is huge, with clothing making up 79% of the country's exports.

On my drive to Rana Plaza, Saif had pointed out the countless city blocks that housed clothing factories. None of them looked remotely like what the school textbooks would have you believe a clothing factory would look like. There was no big chimney, no signage, nothing from the outside to distinguish them from the offices and apartment blocks that stood around them. Saif has spent the last decade of his life working to improve conditions for workers in Bangladesh's clothing industry. He has a very personal stake in it: many of his friends work there. They are among the millions of Bangladeshis who spend their working days making clothes for Western brands. The vast majority are women or children, whose nimble, smaller fingers allow them to do the delicate work.

As I looked around the heart of the Bangladesh clothing sector, it was hard not to feel overcome with anger at just how utterly crazy and unjust the fast fashion world is. If Saif felt the same frustration and dismay as I did about the scene around us, he did not show it. Instead, his optimism was nothing short of inspirational. He was determined to keep working to bring positive changes to the clothing sector in his country. The livelihoods, and lives, of millions of Bangladeshis are dependent on voices like his.

Yet, while I wanted to have the same optimism as Saif, what shocked me most was the fact that the horrific building conditions at Rana Plaza were not unique. It was reported that only six of the 20,000 buildings constructed in Dhaka, (the capital city of Bangladesh) in the five years prior to the Rana Plaza disaster were given the final safety clearance certificates required by law. Though new laws require building owners to apply for such certificates or risk losing water and electricity connections, many building owners neglect to comply. They know that while their buildings are non-compliant, many inspectors and authorities fail to enforce these rules.

Rana Plaza was severely overcrowded. It was well in excess of its maximum occupation requirements, and it was not built according to its blueprints or used for its stated purposes. While it remains the most catastrophic disaster in the history of the garment industry, the sad fact is that it was but one in a long series of clothing factory disasters. The end result of these disasters is a well known reality. Human suffering and needless death is a price that the clothing sector is willing to pay. Each disaster has the same theme: the time was finally up on a ticking time bomb. The list is tragically long. Here are just a few examples:

○   In December 2010, twenty-nine workers died in a factory fire at the 'That's It Sportswear' factory in Dhaka. They were supplying clothes for JC Penney, Gap, Abercrombie & Fitch, and other mainstream brands. The factory was considered modern, but the fire was reportedly triggered by a short-circuit and inadequately installed electrical wiring. Reports indicated that the exits had been blocked and that the factory had never carried out fire drills. Building permits had only been granted for construction of the lower floors. The fire broke out on the ninth floor, which firefighters could not reach because their ladders did not extend beyond the fifth floor. Helicopters could not land on the roof because it had been converted into an illegal cafe. Unionising had been discouraged, preventing workers from collectively addressing concerns with the safety violations. Many of the deceased fell or jumped to their deaths.

○   Almost two years later in November 2012 in Dhaka, 117 people died in a fire in a garment factory operated by Tazreen Fashions. They supplied brands such as Ikea, Disney and Wal-Mart (who own the supermarket chain Asda, selling as George in the UK). The Tazreen factory had been given a high risk safety rating some eighteen months earlier in an audit conducted by an ethical sourcing assessor for Wal-Mart. Still, it continued to operate and produced for the very same brands who had had the factory assessed as high risk. It was a known fact that the building had no emergency exits. This negligence directly resulted in over 100 deaths.

○   In January 2013, seven women died in another factory fire in Dhaka; injured victims included a 15- year-old child. The plant was reportedly operating without clearance from the fire department. This building had fire exits, but it was reported that when the fire started, the workers escape was blocked by locked emergency exits. Tragically, this is a some-what common business practice, where factory owners often employ security staff to prevent workers from taking unau-thorised breaks or stealing from the factory. Many security guards find it easier to lock the exit doors or gates rather than guard the workers. The cultural acceptability of this situation is shocking and heartbreaking.

On my first trip to Bangladesh, I met a man who owns several factories in India. He has a friend who locks the door of the factory and doesn't let the workers leave until they have fulfilled a clothing order. He is an older man who has been in the business for a long time. He sees absolutely nothing wrong with this. He doesn't even try to hide it.

Despite some forward movement from Western brands using Bangladeshi factories after Rana Plaza, the country's safety record is still woefully lacking. Factories overstuffed with hot machinery and fabrics are tinder boxes just waiting to explode. It's the highly flammable lint that we catch in the dryer machine at home, but just on a massively bigger scale, with openly exposed hot wires which are a regular sight at many factories. Unauthorised construction and sealed off exits mean that industrial accidents will continue to injure and kill workers.

Six months after the Rana Plaza disaster, a fire at the Aswad garment factory in Bangladesh killed ten people, even though the fire had started after the factory was closed. Trapped inside were garment workers working overtime in order to meet production deadlines for mainstream brands.

While the clothing brands can reclaim their losses on insurance, the relatives of the dead workers have had to fight relentlessly for any sort of compensation. Families had to wait years before receiving minimal compensation after the Rana Plaza building collapse. It is a scene of injustice that plays out over and over again across the world. The distance between the strong and the weak, the rich and the poor, the West and the rest, seems to grow and grow and grow.

When the fire at the Tazreen Fashions factory in Bangladesh broke out on November 24th 2012, it was reported that a massive clothing order was due for completion that same day. Management had been given strict instructions to not let workers leave the building until the order was completed, something that they continued to enforce even after the fire alarms sounded. Some exits were locked. Others were blocked by large cartons stacked high as the factory rushed to fulfil the order.

In May 2015, a fire engulfed a flip-flop factory in the Philippines, killing 72 people inside. There would have been more survivors had the windows on the second floor not been fitted with iron bars; another common practice meant to prevent theft but that also prevented workers from escaping in the event of an emergency. One worker told reporters that she had never been involved in a fire drill in five years of working at that factory.

More recently, since we started writing this book, oppressive conditions continue to exist all around the globe. CleanClothes.org outlines 114 incidents since January 2021, with 231 workers dying and over 800 individuals being injured. The list is painfully long.

Will conditions improve? Factory owners want to make money. Safety measures cost money. In the words of a Bangladeshi factory owner:

"Many factory owners want to maximise profits, so they will cut corners on safety issues, on ventilation, and on sanitation. They will not pay overtime or offer assistance in case of injuries. They will not build fire exits or stock fire extinguishers. Many of them treat their workers like slaves."

Bottom line, it all comes down to expense, and who is prepared to pay for that cost.

Reframing The Idea of Choice

When we decided to buy only ethically made clothes, we were limiting our choices to less than 0.5% (or something similarly tiny!) of the clothes available in any specific clothing category. Narrowing our options down is not a natural or easy thing to do. But ultimately, we were limiting our options because we had made one choice that trumped all: the choice to live out the values that we held dear. **We made a choice to value the person making our clothes more than the clothes themselves. We made a choice to limit our 'freedoms' in the belief that it might increase the liberties of someone else.** Like many others who walk this path, we chose not to be bystanders. We decided not to take our shopping cues from societal norms, but to choose our own, more values-aligned journey. Turns out it was a much better path. We were surprised and delighted by the choices that we were able to make. Additionally, as we reframed the question of 'choice': we chose to be part of the degrowth, values-aligned mindset.

5

Someone pays: But #2 - But its too expensive

Most of us hate the thought of being ripped off, scammed, or shafted out of our money. We all want to get the best value we can for the goods that we buy. After all, it's our money. We are entitled to have what we have worked for, and most likely, it's been hard-earned. Therefore we want to make sure that we use it as effectively as we can. Additionally, for many of us who view our money through a justice lens, there is often an obligation or sometimes a burden to be a wise and responsible steward of the resources with which we have been blessed. Even if we're not feeling any obligation, we only have the finite amount of money that we have and we have to decide for ourselves how to use it. Besides, there's nothing quite like the feeling of getting a good deal, however we want to define the word 'deal'. As shoppers, we've become hard-wired for it.

We are bombarded with comparison websites, discount codes, Christmas and Black Friday sales. The flashy coupons and sensational

TV or social media ads are all there to tap into our desire for the adrenaline rush of consumption, promising us an even better high when we get something for less money than it's perceived worth. We've all been in conversations where we've heard people boasting about the deal they got on this or that. Who doesn't love to respond to a compliment on their new outfit by bragging, casually adding that they got it for a fantastic price?

There can even be a bit of a stigma that comes with paying full price or over the odds with being the sucker that actually pays the asking price. We might not want to be known as a tight-fisted, Ebenezer Scrooge-style negotiator, but nor do we want to look weak or seem like a pushover. Nobody wants to be the sucker who paid more than they had to. Even if no-one else knows the specific details about a transaction, our money and how we choose to spend it tells us and the world around us a lot about ourselves. It relates to who we aspire to be as well as the reality of what we truly value – publicly and privately. With the incredible economic growth experienced over the majority of the planet since the end of the Second World War, our expectations about our rights and our freedoms with money are unparalleled in human history.

The Contradiction of Spending Money to 'Save' Money

Yet, when our grandparents talked about saving money, they were talking about putting it away in the bank. When we talk about saving money, we're often talking about the gap between what something 'should' have sold for and what we actually bought it for. Spent money is not saved money. Tied into our modern society's different approach to saving, there is also a different approach to investing. Historically, when consumers were making decisions to spend money, they were looking to make a long-term investment in the items they purchased. They expected their investments to last a long time, or perhaps even a lifetime. Consumers across generations understood the difference between products that were going to depreciate in value and those that were going to appreciate, or at least remain stable.

After the unparalleled economic growth of the last 70 years, we now have the expectation that by making thoughtful choices, money invested now will more than likely increase in value over time. While some things are guaranteed to depreciate, we often try to mitigate that. For example we might avoid buying a brand new car as we know it will lose a large percentage of value the minute it is sold.

Additionally, there is often the belief that immediate satisfaction is our right as part of the unparalleled spending culture. It's impossible to function in society today without making short term financial decisions, and yet the extremes that consumers now go to are having devastating impacts on people and on the sustainability of the planet. The prevalence of unsustainable spending lifestyles are all around us. While there are gradually more options to break out of societal norms, such as bringing shopping bags on a trip to a supermarket rather than single use products, incredibly wasteful consumption-based living is still the norm.

As life becomes more and more convenient for many wealthy individuals, the willingness to put up with certain hardships diminishes. This extends across many sectors of life, but has an especially powerful effect in the clothing sector. Much of these changes are logical, understandable and outside of our control. However, this insatiable demand for more, more, more has created incredibly fertile ground to the powers behind fast fashion. It's one thing to maximise the opportunity and try to create value that hasn't been created. It's another matter to cross over into exploiting and manipulating people with the goal of taking value directly at the expense of someone else.

If the 'pie' of wealth is made bigger, which it is when more value is created, then there is an opportunity for wealth to be maximised and enjoyed by all those who have a stake in the pie. However, too often there is a scarcity mentality that results in a 'zero-sum' game. The only growth is at the direct expense of another stakeholder. The most powerful stakeholder will gain value, while the weaker stakeholders will experience a reduction in value and all the negative consequences that go with that. Exploitative capitalism rewards the few while crushing the many.

If win-win scenarios are not being created by the wealthy powerful, then other forces need to ensure that the outcome is something that society is prepared to live with. There is huge variation in what is considered fair or exploitative government regulation. When there is a lack of appropriate government regulations or oversight, society steps in, in various other ways. This can be seen in charity, philanthropic or socially focused endeavours that provide a safety net or opportunities for people to break out of the cycle of poverty.

In many situations in life, unstated cultural norms are the backbone of society. The fact that most neighbourhoods don't have music blaring at 3 am has more to do with societal norms than with the cops being called out to regulate a noise violation dispute. **Society regulates itself with the laws of the land, but also the cultural norms that form expectations and responsibilities that society abides by. Yet, in the clothing sector, fast fashion has completely rewritten the culturally acceptable norms in the last couple of decades.**

The clothing business today is unrecognisable from what it was in our parents' or grandparents' day. How can we possibly claim that we 'can't afford' full-price clothes when for the vast majority of Western consumers, the amount we spend on clothes has massively decreased? We might not want to make the choices that require us to pay what a product is worth, but for most westerns with a certain wealth level, it's our choice and preference rather than a 'can't'.

Is Underwear Really Necessary?

Ironically, when we first started talking about ditching our entire wardrobes, we'd not been focused on one crucial part of attire: underwear. They are a pretty essential basic, alongside, say, socks, unless you're a lot more adventurous and embracing of freedom than we were. Though I expected fair trade boxers to be pricier than the cotton six-packs from the local department store, I was not expecting a pair of boxers to set me back more than I had spent on my wife's Christmas present. (Just kidding. Sort of.)

For only £25 I could get a nice quality pair of fairly-made boxer shorts. One pair. When the realisation started to hit, I started to panic. If a pair of boxers was going to cost me that much, how would I ever be able to afford the rest of my clothes? Setting aside the enormous cost, how could I live with myself for deliberately overlooking a dozen other bargains? Put another way, if I knew I could buy a six-pack at the local department store for £10, how could I, in clear conscience, spend more than twice that for one pair? However, we were committed and had to follow through on the plan. But it was playing with our brains and comfort-level more than we expected.

We'd hid behind the cost 'But' for years, which is why, for us, we felt we simply had to go all in. We picked New Year's Day to purge, because it seemed like the best way to kick-off this massive resolution. Because it's easier to fork out £25 for a pair of boxers if you know that pretty soon you won't have any!

We All Love a Bargain?

We have been culturally encouraged to love a bargain. Whether it's collecting tokens or coupons from newspapers; grabbing a drink - or two - at Happy Hour; finding a hot Groupon deal; or googling discount codes before we buy something online, we love a good deal. A deal is made all the sweeter when we have the feeling of 'getting one over on the man'. We're conditioned to believe that when we 'save' money by getting a deal, the cost is being passed on to the proverbial big corporation. The truth, of course, is much messier. **In the clothing industry, that discount rarely comes out of the pockets of the business owners. Instead, it's the workers footing the bill, both in terms of lower wages as well as in a greatly reduced quality of life.**

When it comes to the hunt for the bargain, we have always been serious players. We enjoyed the 'savings' and the opportunity for a good brag about how clever we were to get a win. When we were at university together, the local supermarket put on an amazing offer: a pack of four orange juice cartons for just £1. Insane! Such a deal. It was substantially below what we would normally pay for orange juice and everyone knows a daily glass of orange juice gives you carte blanche to eat or drink whatever other poor student rubbish you want. Whether scientific data agrees with us or not, we both knew that it was the best preventive medicine to avoid getting ill.

So, when the supermarket put on the offer, I was ready to be focused and maximise my gains. I packed as many cartons into my shopping basket as I could physically carry, only to find out when I was about to pay for it that the deal had a limit: only three sets of OJ per customer. Alas, I could therefore only take 12 cartons in one transaction, so I had to put some back. Undeterred, I went out of my way to go back two or three times a day to the supermarket for the remainder of that week just for the juice, tactically varying shifts and picking a different cashier each time so as not to raise suspicions. Though I spent a small fortune, I could justify the expense by calling it an investment. I ended up accumulating a table-sized stack of orange juice cartons - cleverly disguised by my bed sheet-style tablecloth. I felt pretty smug having saved a fortune in the process!

I started drinking more orange juice than I've ever drunk in my life, and it still took me the remainder of that semester to work my way through that stuff. I have never been so sick of anything in my life. Yet, true to form, I made sure that I and the friends who I was generous enough to share it with, drank every last drop. While I appreciated the healing qualities of the OJ, it wasn't the juice I really wanted. It was the satisfaction of maximising and exploiting the bargain, an absurd but gratifying victory.

I expect that we've all been guilty of bargain-boasting to one degree or another, either privately in our heads or foolishly spoken out loud like I just did. Half the time, we do it to justify having spent money on something we didn't really need in the first place. We justify and defend our overindulgence. **But what if we learned to celebrate fairness in the same way that we celebrate a bargain? Wouldn't fairness eventually come to mean more to people than getting a good deal?**

It's intriguing that philanthropy or charitable giving is often celebrated, be it through plaques on walls or applause and praise at a fundraising event or gala. Yet, what would society look like if we didn't need to have so much celebration of giving money away but instead, if people were generous and fair at the outset? Rather than exploiting and then giving back, what if it was a societal norm to just do the right thing from the start and pay a fair price for things? Personally, I have loved the change from bragging about getting a bargain on a product to bragging about knowing the source and the value of the product. Instead of being focused on a bargain obtained at the expense of someone else, it feels great to focus on the benefits to someone else, even if it comes at some expense to me.

Who Pays the Real Cost of our Savings?

The fashion industry is inextricably linked to bargains. Let's face it, bargain culture is not just limited to shopping the 'sales' in certain seasons. Walk down any main street any day of the year and it seems like most clothes shops are running some sort of sale. It's normally smoke and mirrors, of course. By putting something on a clearance rack and knocking a few pennies off the price, retailers can often get people to buy things they don't want or need, with little correlation to its actual value. With food, there is always an expiration of the product. I had to drink my OJ before the end of the year or else I would have had to throw it out. Clothing, on the other hand, can sit for a long time with minimal pressure to sell it within a certain timeframe.

While there are lots of similarities with other consumer sectors, for various reasons, other industries don't bargain-worship with the same zeal as the clothing sector. There is no closing-down sale from the team trying to sell you a house. But over the last couple of decades, the people who have made our clothes have become less and less visible and are simply known by a 'Made in...' label. Clothing is where the real deals are today, and as consumers, we've all fallen heads over heels in love with this system.

A clothing product can feel like a better purchase if it's a bargain. Perhaps it is not so much a better purchase that a customer is chasing when looking for a bargain, but a better experience. This is particularly true in the more recent trend of fast fashion and virtually disposable clothing. Things are just so cheap, and so disposable, people intentionally buy more than they need, and don't feel any pressure or moral obligation to wear them many times. Even those people who consistently pay more for a brand new car instead of a second-hand one, or people who would never consider buying the supermarket-brand ketchup rather than an established brand might, still make a beeline for the sales or discount rack at a clothes shop.

However, when it comes to clothes, especially those that are so cheap, who is truly paying the price of our savings? Is it truly possible to consistently make a profit on a £5 t-shirt without someone being exploited? Spoiler alert: No, it's not! Who are we getting the better of? And what is that savings truly worth to us? The only truly flexible cost that can constantly be squeezed are the labour costs.

The Value of Clothes - Quality or Quantity?

As a society we've come to place less and less social value on our clothes. If we buy a cheap jumper in a sale and we never actually wear it, we don't feel so bad because, relatively speaking, it hasn't cost us much, probably only as much as a cheap lunch out. We see something we like, we feel marginally attracted to it, and we buy it, because it costs so little. Clothes have become disposable goods. I remember when I lived in Eastern Europe for a couple of years and was greeted with horrified looks when I would dump my jacket on the floor or haphazardly throw it over the back of a chair. At the time, the notion of disposable clothes hadn't yet wound its way to that part of the world. They had fewer outfits than the average Westerner, and they looked after them really well. It was about quality, not quantity. They treated clothing with respect—one of the many moral standards that has been eroded by fast fashion and mass-manufacturing in sweatshops.

The Baby-Boomer generation have led the charge on this price reduction to the point where Millennials as consumers have only ever known cheap clothes. The fashion industry has instilled in us all a belief that we can - and should - be able to pick up an item for a dirt cheap price. In turn, this has created a culture of throw-away consumption. Younger consumers don't expect to spend much of their budget on clothing. Convincing them to buy a £21 t-shirt when they can pop over to the high street and get one for 75% less will not be easy. It's a shift that many aren't willing to make.

Shelling out £25 for boxers was painful—especially for two blokes that once gamed an orange juice sale. We suffered from the same reservations many Western shoppers would have. Why spend £63 on three fairly made t-shirts, when we could have brought ten similar t-shirts for that same price? It took discipline, and soul-searching, to keep our goals clear. Which would be worse—paying more for a t-shirt or buying something cheaply made by someone getting paid a fraction of minimum wage to make it? **There was a cost to our savings, and it was real human beings that were shouldering it.**

There were some things we didn't buy, simply because we didn't feel we could afford them. Our friend Johnald decided to drop a few quid and got himself some really nice, ethically sourced boxer shorts made from organic bamboo. He told us about the shorts on a daily basis and regularly offered to model them for us as they were apparently unbelievably soft and cosy. We both got boxer envy. We had never worn clothes made from bamboo, and had no understanding that the quality was so superb. It wasn't too long before we got on the bamboo boxer-train so we too could enjoy the experience of wearing something so comfortable every day. Those bamboo boxers were worth every penny, proving once again that you get what you pay for.

Everything Else Goes Up While the Price of Clothes Keeps Going Down

Throw-away tops are a new concept. By this, we mean the £3 t-shirt; the three-pack of camisoles for £5. Clothes haven't always been this cheap. Whilst the cost of everything from college fees, housing, utilities, tickets for a night out or even our weekly groceries has gone up over the last 30 years, the cost of clothing has gone down. And it hasn't gone down just by a bit, but by a lot.

Back in the 1920s, the typical UK customer spent 13-15% of their income on clothing. Today the average consumer spends around 3% on their income on clothing. A household with average income is spending around £780 a year on clothes – considerably cheaper than the £3,380-£3,900 we'd be spending if we had maintained the 1920s spending proportion. Clothing appears to be one of the only mass-consumed items in our culture that hasn't followed a normal inflation curve. Buying fairly-made clothing requires us to buck against the downward cost trend of clothing.

Making Fair Affordable Means Supporting Smaller Brands

We discovered along our journey that many of the ethical brands we bought from when replenishing our wardrobes seemed to be charging more than a certain percentage extra for the privilege of buying fairly made clothes. The £25 price tag on boxers, for example, seemed like too much for some sort of ethical levy. We genuinely weren't sure if the ethical brands were forcing an unreasonable profit, or whether they truly had to charge those prices in order to cover their operating costs.

We won't deny that fairly-made clothes are more expensive to produce and to buy. Logically, treating workers obviously costs more money. Paying for ethical sourcing as well as customer experience for a low volume business costs money. But does that mean that ethically made clothes are truly not affordable? Or, put another way, is it impossible to convince people that being ethical is worth the price?

Unfortunately, ethically made products, whether clothing or coffee, cost more to produce, and that cost is virtually always passed on to the consumer. This means that lower-income consumers are not financially able to buy ethically. So long as large manufacturers and retailers control the market, ethical companies cannot possibly compete at scale. But this doesn't mean that it is hopeless. We found that for many people, the increased cost of buying ethically is very feasible.

There's a nuance between what is expensive, and what is afford-able. Cars are expensive. But many of us are able to afford some kind of car. Going out for dinner is typically more expensive than eating in. But many of us make decisions with our budgets to ensure that we can eat out, even if it's just once every couple of months. Every time we buy a latte at a coffee shop, we are making the decision to spend more on something that we could obtain cheaper else-where. So why the resistance to pricing in our clothing purchases? Why is there such a discrepancy between those who say they care about ethical clothing and those who are actually prepared to spend more on it?

What if we paid more for our clothes, bought fewer of them, and took better care of them so that they lasted longer? What if we decided that instead of comparing the price of fairly-made clothes to those made in places like Rana Plaza, we instead compared, relatively, our clothing budget to the budgets of families in the 1920s? **What if, rather than prioritising the bargain, we prioritised fairness? What if we took a step back and re-flected on history and the modern day horrific consequences being experienced today by garment workers?**

Perhaps if we asked these questions, our view of what things really cost would change. What is the reality of the situation faced by a sweatshop worker?

Non-Living Wage

It's truly hard to comprehend the income challenges and experiences of someone who has been born into the trap of extreme poverty. Empathy is paramount for understanding the reality of what others are going through, and data provides some objectivity to the experience. The numbers revealed the harsh reality of the situation and helped us to be empathetic to a reality that we knew so little about.

In December 2013, in response to increasing global scrutiny of the clothing industry, the Bangladeshi government increased the minimum wage for entry-level garment workers from 3,000 takas a month ($38 USD), to Tk. 5,300 ($68 USD). One might like to think that's acceptable due to the context and the fact that things always seem cheaper in developing economies, based on our experiences of traveling overseas where we enjoy the advantage of seeing our money go a lot further. However, even with the reality that some things are cheaper in developing economies, it is shocking just how hard it is for people to make ends meet on less than $100 a month.

A few months before the wage hike announcement, a Bangladeshi think-tank, the Centre for Policy Dialogue (CPD) offered the Government three levels upon which to base a minimum wage for garment workers. The lowest wage option would be an improvement on existing conditions, but still keep workers below the poverty line, eating fewer calories than they would need to get through a day at the factory. The middle option would allow them to meet basic living costs. Only the highest pay option would allow them to afford a diet meeting the various required allowances for energy, carbohydrates and vitamins.

The new minimum wage implemented was less than the lowest option proposed by the CPD. The result was **Bangladeshi factory workers are consistently paid well below what they need in order to be able to afford food that would meet the most basic nutritional needs.** Perhaps this should not have been surprising when approximately thirty of the country's Members of Parliament (MPs or legislators) or around 10%, own and operate clothing factories.

The reality is that garment workers in many emerging markets (developing countries, Global South or whatever name is most appropriate to describe countries with a lower than average GDP) cannot afford a diet with sufficient calories. In Sri Lanka, a Labour Department survey found that 66% of female workers in the clothing industry had anaemia. In Cambodia, one in three garment workers are medically underweight. These workers simply are not paid enough to afford basic nutrition.

Sadly, having a minimum wage enshrined in law – even one that doesn't pay you enough to escape poverty – is still no guarantee that you will actually receive it. In the Centre for Policy Dialogue's research into wages, they noticed that in every single case study, the wages being reported by Bangladeshi workers were lower than those being reported to Western buyers. In Vietnam, a full quarter of factories aren't paying their staff the minimum wage, despite the fact that it is regulated by law.

Consistent Payday Delays & Extreme Poverty

Beyond the ridiculously low wage amount, when it comes to pay, another problem facing many garment workers across the world is that there is consistently a question whether they will be paid that meagre wage on time, or at all. Consistently late pay is prevalent across the clothing industry and one of the biggest and often unspoken challenges for the workers. A lack of a reliable and consistent payment schedule means that things which we take for granted, like planning when to buy food or schoolbooks, or knowing when you can take your kids to see the doctor for a check up, becomes even more complicated and in some cases, impossible.

As one garment worker noted:

"The managers say they will pay us on the 10th of every month but sometimes they give it on the 12th, or maybe the 14th, or even after the 20th. Last month we got our salaries on the 22nd. But we still have to pay our rent in the first week of every month, pay for food and send money home to our parents".

While we as consumers crave choice, we will only consider it a 'choice' if it is at an acceptable expense point for us. Its hard, if not impossible for most of us to even begin to understand the challenges of extreme poverty. A cost needs to be paid for a product and if we are not prepared to pay an appropriate price for a product, then invariably those who make the product are bearing that cost instead.

6

Wearing our identity: But #3 – But I want to look good

Honestly, when we first jumped into this whole thing, one of our concerns was that we would have to dress like hippies. In our minds, ethical clothing was synonymous with boho-chic - worn by people who not only didn't seem to care how they looked, but actively seemed to fight mainstream fashion and embrace looking 'different'. Most of the people we'd met who said they were committed to buying clothes that had been made fairly looked like they'd just returned from a year-long backpacking trip and were wearing all their souvenirs. We've both been on foreign holidays and bought ponchos and straw hats that seemed perfectly normal for the place that we were in, only to realise that we felt awkward and out of place wearing those items back home.

Through our ethical clothing journey, we came to believe that buying ethically made clothes made us somewhat subversive, and we were curious to find out what that was going to mean for us long term. But we still wanted to wear clothes consistent with our own cultures and personal styles. We were never going to be fashion models, but hoped that we could still look somewhat pulled-together and professional by Western standards when the need arose.

When we told people about our plans to give away all our clothes and wear only ethically made clothes, some of the reactions were extreme. One person asked us if we were going to become "one of those people who swallows swords and treks around India to find their Zen". We hadn't planned on that, but, we understood why people conjured up these images in their heads. We'd only ever met a few people who were 100% committed to only owning ethical fashion, and for most of them it meant wearing clothes that weren't made in factories, but by individual artisans. Given the abuses suffered by many garment workers in factories, we understand why some people would choose to pay a premium for something made by an artisan. Beyond just being ethical, artisan designs can be a great way to support the preservation of ancestral skills. However, focusing on artisan clothing wasn't the purpose of our project. And in many cases, individually artisan-made clothes are representations of another culture and not intended to be worn in the professional Western-world context.

Clothes Reflect Our Identity

When we gave away our clothes, we discovered we had a strong emotional attachment to a number of items. Mostly it reminded us of occasions when we had worn the clothes, or parallel events going on in the world at the time we bought those clothes. Very occasionally we remembered the feeling that we had when we acquired a specific item. Yet our understanding as to how much clothes reflect our identity became even clearer when we gave these memory-laden clothes away.

I mentioned earlier the 'Dress for Success' program being run in the local prison, where donated professional clothing is given to inmates upon their release in an effort to ease their transitions back into the workforce. The obvious suddenly became clear: the worth of those outfits was way more than any monetary value to the men receiving them. Giving away my suits to people who could use them to increase their chances of getting a job was a clear reminder of the inherent social value of the clothes that we wear. Those suits became a visual representation of changed lives, and were very influential for the world's perception of the man wearing them. For me, this underscored the importance of the fact that, beyond showing or disguising our shape or flattering our figure, clothes show who we are to the society around us.

As we considered whether to tell people about our new clothing commitment or remain silent, it was impossible not to think about how much our clothes reflected our identity. We wanted to avoid being pious and challenging everyone else on their clothing purchasing decisions. It felt amazing to have the satisfaction of knowing our money had purchased more than just a piece of fabric; it also made a difference in someone's life. There was no pumping of our chests and no outward appearances that we were any different from the rest of society. Yet, we felt a definite difference inside, knowing that what we wore now reflected who we wanted to be.

Finding business attire, and specifically a mainstream suit jacket, proved to be incredibly hard. Fortunately, I was eventually able to get one custom made. Early on in the journey, as we entered one particular meeting at our lawyer's office, it became clear that this wasn't dress-down Friday and that only one of us, thankfully me, had a suitable jacket. Even though we were somewhat different sizes and even though Andy had changed his shape a little with fatherhood, we realised that we had to find a way to share the jacket. As the partners and rest of the legal team came in and out for the meet and greet, we managed to take the one jacket that we had and by strategically wearing it, and hanging it on the back of one chair and then on another, we managed to somehow present the appearance of both of us having suits. I'm pretty confident that no one else in the room noticed. It's a silly story, but it showed us just how much clothing helped to create an impression, including impressions that were sometimes blatantly false.

The Legendary Tunic

Undoubtedly, my most unfortunate clothing purchase was a tunic crafted by an artisan in Asia, which I purchased online. I had left it perilously close to the January deadline for completing the wardrobe reboot, and was running the risk of not having a single long sleeve top to wear in a week's time. It was already cold. Not only was I in the midst of the 'panic before Christmas of 2013', but there was the reality of the fact that winter was coming! I bought the tunic from a co-operative of local artisans and was pleased to have found something - anything - to wear on those confusing warm/semi-cold days when there is a need to cross the gap between a t-shirt and wool sweater. The story of the impact on the worker was compelling, and while I would never have paid the price I did for a long sleeve t-shirt twelve months earlier, I needed something quickly, and I purchased it out of desperation, rather than thoughtful reflection. At this stage, I wasn't focused on the 'compliment competition'. I just needed something.

The tunic came in two different sizes – big and small. The tight V-neck cascaded down, tent-like, to form a sort of base of a cone around my waist. Even the arms were funnel-shaped, the sleeves fanning out like 1970s flares but on my arms rather than my feet.

It was less t-shirt and more teepee. To top it all off, it came only in brown, not an unwearable colour, but still one more commonly associated with stains in the clothing context than anything else.

I cringe, looking back now on how in my desperation to buy something quickly, I missed out on all the obvious clues that this purchase was not going to work out well. It's safe to say that, from a quick look on the co-operative's website, they had not paid top dollar for the man-next-door picture of the 'model' wearing the tunic. The website's own marketing copy was peppered with phrases like "each style has a unique fit," (aka we don't believe in traditional size charts) and "many people who encounter our products say that the fabrics carry an energy with them," (aka we haven't invested in quality control). And my personal favourite: "'The vibrant colours of the block printed fabrics and the skill of the embroidery are unlike the garments we so often encounter in North America today" (no guarantees!). The writing was on the wall.

Initially, I was oblivious. It was a style that was totally in keeping in the locale from whence it came, but somewhere, in my pursuit of fairness, I had been blinded to the fashion norms of my own culture. Even when the tunic arrived in the post, in all its tent-like glory, I was still ignorant of the crime against fashion that I was committing. It was only when my wife came home from work that reality set in. She refused to speak to me until I had changed out of the tunic. It went into the laundry pile having been worn for a mere 30 minutes. The hope was, similar to washing your hair immediately after a shocking haircut, that by putting it through a cycle in the washing machine it would somehow soften into a new, semi-fashionable, or at least wearable without embarrassment, item. Alas, it was not to be.

I write this with no intent to disrespect local cultures or fashions. Our ethical journey was rooted in our commitment to buy clothes specifically from manufacturers in the developing world. But since we live in the West and wanted to demonstrate that it was possible to buy fair trade and still wear clothes that fit into our own cultural norms, we had to be realistic about how some ethnic styles translated into Western markets. The early answer on this tunic was: not well.

In those early days whilst awaiting some more sensible ethical buys to arrive, I was actually quite glad of the tunic. I was fortunate to be working from home at the time and so no-one needed to know what I was wearing. I had one tidy V-neck which worked just fine for video calls, as long as I remembered to position the camera correctly. But for people who have jobs requiring professional attire, for daily wear, the challenge of finding fair and fashionable clothes suitable for work is a very real one. It is an area in which the ethical clothing sector is in dire need of growth. We tucked this challenge away for later consideration.

As I said, when we first jumped into this whole thing, one of our concerns was that we were going to have to dress like hippies, and the tunic incident did nothing to allay these concerns. We had the mistaken belief that ethical clothing was never going to really look good. It took us each more than 50 hours to restock our wardrobes, 150 hours in total. This included research, searching and ordering online, and returning items that didn't fit. We found that we could easily spend three hours online trying to find a single shirt. Relatively speaking, that was way more time shopping than we had ever spent before; an enormous time investment that many people can't afford to make. Thankfully, in the last decade there has been tremendous progress in compiling lists of recommended brands, so you won't need to spend as long as we did!

At the time, we needed to remind ourselves that this minor effort of inconvenience was nothing compared to the wider problem of horrific working conditions in the sector that we wanted to see abolished. Every time we asked ourselves, "Am I committed enough to my values to persevere with this shopping experience?", the answer was a simple "Yes" and then a review of another ethical brand.

The reality was that this method of shopping was new and different to us, and was made more challenging by the desperation we felt to replace an entire wardrobe in a matter of months. I had wasted plenty of time in the past driving to a big box store full of sweatshop-made products, just to buy a single item. Many of us do this when we feel like it, without really thinking about. We drive across town to get something at the only IKEA around, go miles out of our way to eat at our favourite fast food restaurant, or even travel across a border for cheaper food or alcohol. We do all these things with minimal complaint or consideration. Spending time online shopping was just something we had to get used to, and with a little patience and perseverance, we became better at it and comfortable with it. It was simply a matter of perspective and commitment.

While we joked about 'The Tunic', it was well made, even if its exuberant design meant that I didn't feel comfortable and confident wearing it out in public, but honestly, my feelings towards the tunic were mostly about the fact that I was so keen to avoid the stereo-typical look of fair trade clothing. We all care about how we dress, both from a design perspective and from the desire to look like we have our lives together or other parts of our personality that we're trying to represent. With the wisdom gained over the journey, we ended up becoming more strategic shoppers and having greater confidence in our purchasing decisions. As it turned out, we got more compliments on our limited but intentionally selected ward-robes than we ever had received before. **Apparently we could look good by buying good. And, knowing that we were having a positive impact greatly added to the feel-good factor.**

7

The undeniable truth: But #4 - But is there any real impact?

Over the last few decades, clothes have come to have less value for consumers. Arguably, with globalisation and a huge physical distance between buyers and producers, consumers are becoming ever less discerning about where their clothes come from. For social justice-minded customers, smart marketers have exploited this with fast growth and the socially acceptable 'give back' culture. While sometimes having good intentions and positive impact, too often, the basic premise of 'taking' (or disguised by the word 'winning') and then 'giving back' (sometimes disguised by claiming to be 'charity') is the acceptable way of doing business. What exploitation have we become accustomed to accepting? Even worse, what exploitation have we accepted with the belief that it is charity's job to fix the negative consequences of that exploitation? What if we turned things on their head? What if we changed our whole view on impact so that there was no need to 'give back'?

The Triangle Factory and the Migration of the Sweatshop

Another tragic accident, with many similarities to Rana Plaza, occurred at the Triangle garment factory. Reportedly, a fabric scrap bin unexpectedly went up in flames. There were no fire alarms, so workers on the ninth floor were doomed, they did not even know about the fire until the flames came barreling towards them. The owners had locked the workers inside to stop them from stealing. The exits were blocked, and the porter who held the key had already escaped. The building had a single, rickety fire escape ladder. Because the construction was so shoddy, it crumpled under the weight of those trying to use it, hurtling around twenty people to their deaths on the cold road, a hundred feet below. In total, 146 people died, most from the fire, but many from jumping or falling off the building in an effort to escape. Of those who died, 123 were women - some as young as 14 years old.

Here's what is different about this tragedy than the others that we have mentioned previously. This factory was located in Manhattan, USA. The year was 1911.

Sweatshops are not a new phenomenon but are now virtually non-existent in the West. However, it was only a few generations ago that garment workers in places like New York were facing many of the same horrific conditions that many in emerging markets face today. On August 1 1938, the American periodical Life Magazine boldly declared, *"Thirty years ago the industry stank of the sweatshop and the cruellest kind of exploitation ...Still numerous in 1933, the sweatshop is virtually gone today".* Although there are many ways that manufacturing factories are still abusive in the West, Western society has moved to the point that sweatshops must be obscured from view and operated through thoroughly illegal processes. The last century has seen factory conditions improve beyond recognition for much of the Western world. Unfortunately, the new generation of factories that have sprung up in emerging markets are replicating the tragic catastrophes of the early industrial revolution in the UK and tragedies like the 1911 Triangle Factory disaster in New York.

So, while sweatshops are not new, the outsourcing of our clothing manufacturing to emerging markets is new and part of a more modern trend. Even as recently as 2010, Europe still produced the majority of the world's clothes, as it had done since the eighteenth century. But in the first decade of this millennium, it was reported that the UK lost two-thirds of its textiles and clothing jobs. Since 2005, 80% of jobs in the textile, clothing, leather and footwear industries in the United States have moved overseas. At the same time, from 2004 to 2008, employment in the clothing industry in Bangladesh alone increased by 40%. In Vietnam, it shot up by 52%. Jobs in the clothing industry have been outsourced to developing countries, and concurrently, the price of what we wear has come down. The cost of this in human suffering has been incalculable.

Is It Really That Bad?

Are things really as awful as we're making them out to be? We both remember growing up in the U.K. on a sporadic diet of stories about Nike sweatshops, which we don't seem to hear about anymore. Child labour, which used to be in the news fairly regularly, is rarely reported on today. So have things improved, or does it just seem that way?

In 2013, the International Labour Organisation reported that child labour was down by a third since the year 2000. At first glance, this sounds like a positive statistic. **However, the scope of the**

problem is so enormous that there are still 168 million children trapped in horrific work conditions. At least 168,000,000 children are being deprived of a childhood that they can never recover. 168,000,000 children are working in factories and farms to produce dirt-cheap goods, mostly for a Western market in search of dramatically discounted clothes. That's more than twice the number of children living in the United States. That's more than the entire adult and child populations of the UK, Italy and Spain combined.

So while there has definitely been some progress in recent years, it hasn't yet made a dent in the global problem. As public awareness has reached new heights, **many mainstream brands have simply gotten more adept at hiding the reality, rather than addressing and correcting the issue.** The intentional murkiness of global supply chains has increased.

In the last twenty years, we have seen the rise of Corporate Social Responsibility (CSR). It has become a 'must have' for many respectable institutions. But what sounds like a great development for more businesses to be doing the right thing can often be boiled down to simply a clever spin for marketing teams, aiming to sell their brands as paragons of corporate ethics. Many brands' marketing departments specialise in keeping the bad stuff out of the news, and putting the good stuff in. Whether it's planting trees in Haiti or buying textbooks in Mali, brands love to talk about the positive impact that they're having. Mainstream financial institutions love to brag about their generous loans to small business owners and massive investments in the infrastructures of economically poor areas.

Successful CSR teams can offset the amoral costs of unadulterated capitalism with meagre displays of altruism which cost the companies next to nothing. 'Greenwashing', and now increasingly, 'fair-trade washing' are often only used by larger corporate brands to gloss over atrocious business practices. **This practice can be devastating to truly values-driven brands. Intentionally muddying the water makes it harder for a consumer to see the difference between sincere values-driven organisations and those who are only interested in ticking a box.**

Arguably, more often than not, the publicity generated by CSR teams is designed to placate customers rather than to genuinely help the labour force. Some CSR departments spend more money on telling people about their good deeds than on the good deeds themselves, especially when CSR is simply fulfilling the needs of their company's marketing department. Unfortunately, CSR can be one of the main obstacles for growth in the ethical clothing sector. It is a powerful illustration of the distortion in the sector when values aren't aligned and when marketing about the impact becomes more important than the impact itself.

As we dived deeper into the ethical clothing world, on the one hand, it became clear who was green-washing (purporting to save the planet) or pink-washing (purporting to support womens' rights), or fair trade-washing (purporting to be fair when in reality they are not) their companies. It was frustrating to see companies with unashamedly abusive practices use a great marketing or CSR department to make the company appear to be something that it blatantly was not.

Do We Really Want to Know the Truth?

There is no question that brands are using sleight of hand to hide the dark reality from the Western consumer. For us, there was a bigger question looming: Do we really want to know the truth? Or is it just a little bit too uncomfortable?

Take one of our extended family members as an example. He knew how passionate we are about these issues. He had heard us talk about the appalling conditions that many people face in sweat-shops as they go about their daily work. We shared with him the stories and the statistics that you've read in this book. Still, he casually turned to me one day and asked, *"It's not really that bad though, is it? It just can't be"*

We've seen and experienced this conversation time and time again. People hear the facts and learn about the faces behind those facts, and yet still, for various reasons, they refuse to let it sink in. What happens in the production of our clothes happens far away from us, to people we don't personally know, with cultures and languages we know very little about. It's easy to compartmentalise. The label on our t-shirt that simply says 'Made in Bangladesh' doesn't tell the story of a human being. It's easier to refuse to see, or as is the case of my family member, to outright ignore the reality so we can turn a blind eye to it and just carry on as we are. **For a compassionate person, accepting it means doing something about it. And that responsibility can feel like too much.**

Somehow, as a society, we have convinced ourselves that because we care about people, when we hear these awful stories, we need to put them out of our mind, because the responsibility of taking on everyone's suffering is just too much. We don't know how to help. In the digitally connected world, we have become oversaturated with tragedy and feel overwhelmed by it. Even if we do feel compassion, what difference can one person really make anyway? As we'll show in the upcoming chapters, by simply choosing where we buy clothes from, we can have a life-changing impact for those making our clothes.

WHAT ABOUT YOU?

Chances are that you're reading this book because you do care; you care about those who make your clothes, you care about the conditions they face, and you want to see them both paid and treated fairly. You want them to work in conditions that you would be willing to work in. You know that geography doesn't define intrinsic human value. But too often and too easily, we are convinced that, as consumers, we have no responsibility or power over the lives of the people who make our clothes, the very clothes that we are wearing right now! This is not true. **We do have a responsibility and we each have power to move the needle. And it's our belief that, through our buying choices, we all can!**

In the words of one Bangladeshi worker:

"If you buyers just thought for 1 second about what it's like for us workers, the fast fashion industry would reduce by half overnight."

PART II Visible: Our Values-Driven Social Enterprise

8

Creating an online brand: Real due diligence

While at times it had been hard work to do all the research and completely rebuild our wardrobes, it had also been incredibly inspiring. We had become increasingly energised and hopeful about the positive impact that could be achieved in the sector. So many good people were doing incredible and innovative things to change the world. While there was an abundance of critiquing and fault finding to remind us that nothing was perfect, there were loads of pioneering approaches underway, led by committed people and making a profound difference. And yet, we knew that more needed to be done. People had often asked us what more could be done and where they could find the best opportunities to make a difference. We felt we had a moral obligation to respond with a good answer about what we were going to do.

We came to the strong conclusion that one person, one individual, one customer could truly make a difference. Each piece of clothing had a story behind how it was made and we

could either continue to be part of the problem passively by accepting a bad, exploitative story, or we could take responsibility and be part of the solution.

Beyond our personal buying decisions, we wondered whether there was more that we could do in swimming upstream against the powerful tide of fast fashion. Would people listen to us when we suggested ethical companies to buy from? Could we encourage other consumers to pare down their wardrobes? Was there a more effective way for us to help stimulate the ripples of change? If so, what was it?

Out of these questions came the spark of an idea: to launch a business of our own that would provide quality, ethically made, fairly priced clothes. We envisioned a business making clothes that looked good, and delivering excellent service to customers. Nothing flashy, as we still weren't fashionistas, just straightforward, everyday clothes. Our purpose was to directly increase the choices available to people who decided to live out their values through the clothes that they bought. We also hoped that we could have a catalytic impact on other companies and customers in the wider sector by being open and honest about our approach. Since we had come to fervently believe that individuals as customers have the power to impact the situation, we wanted to create more opportunities for people to have a positive impact on the lives of factory workers.

The Genius of Johnald

During our initial wave of conversations about giving away all our clothes and building ethical wardrobes from scratch, we asked our friend John 'Johnald' Payne, to join us on the journey. We'd all met each other while at university and had had a number of adventures together, some more shareable than others. Tragically, Johnald died suddenly in 2016. As we wrote this book, it was a pleasure to remember the deep and meaningful conversations as well as the pure comedy that came from sharing the early part of this journey with him.

Over the years, we had enjoyed multiple conversations with Johnald about everyone's unique role in the world, and how we could best use our gifts and talents to make a positive difference. For someone who loved to banter, Johnald also had a deep and compassionate heart for the most marginalised in our world. He thought a lot about how he could use his analytical and technological skills in parallel with his passion to change the world. As we were deciding on our criteria to rebuild our wardrobes, and critically assessed the brands that we wanted to buy from, Johnald came up with many ideas for how to share our journey with a wider audience.

However, it was on our travels to meet up with potential supply partners that Johnald's overlap of business sense and compassion really shone. As a successful computer scientist, Johnald was well compensated for any web design or programming job that he did. Over the years, he became increasingly selective in choosing what work gigs he took on. With that extra time and freedom, he explored and partnered with social entrepreneurs who were building impactful businesses in various sectors.

One of the things that had connected us with Johanld at university was our mutual loathing of 'faffing'. Faffing refers to the minutes and hours that are wasted while people stand around umming and ahhing, trying to come up with an actionable plan. Because we were action-oriented and wanted to get stuff done, faffing was extremely irritating to us. So, after hours, days, and months of slogging away on desk research, we decided that we needed to stop faffing and take action.

The next step was to learn more about what was actually going on in the clothing sector on the ground. Our initial plan was to meet with ethical manufacturers in the Global South to better understand their business models, their challenges and the wider impact that ethical clothing was having on the world. We hoped to learn in person from the visionary company leaders. We were also keen to connect directly with the people who made our clothes, the individuals who physically worked at the machines to make product and to see if we could collaborate in some way with them.

We worked with Common Objective (formerly known as Ethical Fashion Forum) to connect with a number of companies in their network. We were open about our goal of finding collaborators that we could work, even if we weren't sure exactly what form that would take. We decided our first step would be to find a company with a DNA of fairness that was bringing real change to the lives of the individuals making the clothing and explore how we could connect them better with consumers like us.

It was exciting. We were prepared to step forward into the relatively unknown. We did more desk research and planned out the trip, but with minimal faffing. We were ready to learn by doing. So, Johnald and I packed our bags with all that we needed. Indeed, we took literally *all* the clothes that we owned, and boarded a plane to Asia. We flew to India, a major focal point of the global clothing industry.

Traveling to the Source – Visiting Change Makers

Factory #1 - Looking For a Deeper Connection With The Team

It was 8 am on a sweltering summer morning as we waited outside our hotel. The city was alive and pulsing with activity. Throngs of people noisily and purposefully wove their way through the crowded streets. The stifling air was pierced by the ceaseless honking of car horns. Clothing factories were major employers in this city, as in many other urban centres throughout the country. With over 35 million workers, India's textile industry is the country's second biggest employer behind agriculture. As we waited for our ride, it was fascinating to slow down, to watch the daily hustle.

Sanju, the factory owner we were due to meet, arrived in his well-used Tata truck at five past nine. We jumped in, and joined him on his daily commute to his Fair Trade Certified factory. The first thing that hit us as we walked through the doors of the factory was the noise. The sensory overload was incredible. We'd been to India before so we were well prepared for the incredible blend of sounds and smells, but this was on a different level. It was overwhelming. The factory was at full capacity and was absolutely buzzing. It was a reflection of Sanju's ability to sell clothes that every machine was in use and that each one throughout the open floor plan building seemed to have the volume turned up full.

We were told that there were about 200 people working in the factory, spread out over several floors. Most of the levels did not have separate offices but just one large, open workspace. To help the staff see better, the spaces were brightly lit by powerful but extremely hot fluorescent lights. We saw cutters, sewing machine operators, packers, quality control monitors and line managers.

Most of them were female. All of them were hard at work making hoodies, shirts, women's tops and T-shirts.

In the display room downstairs, away from the din of the machines, we admired the clothing and we were impressed by the quality of their work. The finished products were stacked high, waiting to be transported to shops in the West and into the shopping baskets of people like you and me.

We spent the day with Sanju, touring the various parts of the factory, meeting his team and asking him questions. We asked loads of questions, all of which he was more than willing to answer. He seemed to be a genuinely good bloke who faced the constant pressure of needing to make enough money to sustain his business and eke out a profit, while also maintaining his values. Sanju proudly displayed the various certificates that his company had received as a result of the filings, audits and reporting they had completed to be certified with both Fair Trade USA and Fairtrade International. In order to achieve compliance, Sanju's factory received SA8000 status after completing an audit by Social Accountability International. Their material needed to comply with Global Organic Textile Standards (GOTS) to verify that the clothes they produced were certifiably organic.

We were learning fast and trying to understand what all this meant. Seeing and learning in person was a very different experience compared to the desk research we had previously undertaken. Sanju's factory's certification as ethical by third party evaluators had recently been update. They had had to jump through many hoops, not just to be fair but also to be seen to be fair. As a result, we weren't the only potential buyers visiting him that day. A couple of representatives from a company based in Europe were there as well, as they looked to expand more into organic products.

It was clear from our short visit that Sanju's customer base came from all corners of the world, and he was confident that his base would continue to grow. Sanju believed he was ahead of the curve in the marketplace, telling us that he could see an exponential growth in demand for organic and Fair Trade certified clothes in a variety of Western markets. Because the certification process takes time, and because cotton can't be classed as organic until three years since pesticides were last used, Sanju was hoping to be among the early adopters of clothing manufacturers using organic cotton. While there weren't yet sufficient companies that were looking for 100% organic production, he wanted to be ready to take full advantage when the tide turned.

It was a fantastic start to our trip and we were suitably impressed by the certifications and the lengths that Sanju was prepared to go to meet the fair trade criteria. But while we trusted the certifications and had no reason to question Sanju's values for his business, we felt very removed from the workforce. We weren't able to connect with the team as individuals, to learn more about their personal experience working in a Fair Trade factory. The reliance on third party certification had not only outsourced accountability but seemed to have also outsourced connection opportunities. Still, it was an amazing visit, an incredible work environment and we were eager to learn more.

Factory #2 - Big Players Squeeze Out The New Players

With little time to spare on our journey, early the following morning, we boarded our next plane. We were both buzzing from all that we had just seen. The direct two-hour flight gave us a little time to reflect and discuss what we had learned the day before. Before we knew it, we were landing in Tirupur, arguably the clothing capital of India. With over 80% of Indian exports being produced in the region, there is a deep, longstanding connection to clothing manufacturing.

The second factory we visited had been set up by a religious community who wanted to provide jobs for marginalised people. The company employed around 300 people, many of whom were women from at-risk and low-income communities. At least a third of their workforce was physically challenged or disabled. The value they placed on people also extended to the materials that they used: garments were 100% organic and Fair Trade certified cotton, and at the time of our visit, they were very proud to be 'the only garment manufacturer in India producing solely certified organic garments".

Their holistic approach was designed to encourage sustain-ability at every stage of the production process, both purchasing from farmers who practised fair trade and organic cultivation, and ensuring that their workforce was treated fairly. Their mission was twofold: to serve marginalised populations, and to produce products with minimal negative impact upon the environment. Their commitment to both social and environmental sustainability was inspirational.

At the time we visited, this business that had sprung from a humble seed was celebrating its 20th anniversary. The years of hard work were paying off as their list of clients continued to grow. They were producing clothing for established mainstream retailers such as H&M, Debenhams, Tesco, Topshop and John Lewis.

Unfortunately, when we arrived, the senior management had been called away on an urgent matter, so we were unable to spend much time with them. This was disappointing, but we were de-termined to make the best of our scouting trip. We learned a lot, especially about the competency required to produce for large mainstream brands. We appreciated being able to learn first hand about the opportunities for positive environmental impact.

However, we were shocked by how large the factory's minimum purchase order was. They were playing with the big players and not with newbies like us. There was no way we were going to be able to have a seat at their table until we had a decent sized company.

Factory #3 - Fair Trade Certification Changes Power Dynamics

As expected, there was no shortage of clothing factories in the clothing hub of Tirupur. Intentionally acting on a last minute whim, we called one that was nearby and arranged for an impromptu visit. This was the least researched factory that we visited on the trip, so we weren't sure what to expect when the taxi dropped us off. On one hand, we thought there would be a marked contrast between a factory that didn't position itself as ethical, and the two Fair Trade certified factories that we'd just visited. On the other hand, we weren't surprised to find that, on the outside at least, it looked pretty similar to the other two - clean and presentable.

We were also aware that appearances could be deceiving. We knew that some factories were notoriously skilled at hiding their illicit violations. We wondered how much we could really discern about a factory's commitment to fairness during a cursory viewing of their factory floor with no prior due diligence. The issue of transparency could be further complicated if the factory owner knew in advance that we were considering buying from them; they would most certainly have a vested interest in hiding unsafe and illegal conditions.

We were greeted by one of the managers who was boisterous and friendly. As soon as he'd heard about our visit, he had clearly made us his new priority for the day. We were astonished at the level of attention we had unintentionally commanded. We were mindful of the sacrifice that he and his team were generously making in being so accommodating. We felt like mini-celebrities; they ushered us from room to room with endless offerings of tea and a somewhat uncomfortable deference. As Westerners with money, ready to place an order, we instantly occupied positions of power, despite our humble intentions. There was nothing improper. They were just trying to make a good business decision in a market that doesn't offer them many favours. However, it was easy to see how quickly and easily factory owners would bow to the pricing and timing demands of Western brands, regardless of any negative implications for their workers. For us, it was all rather uncomfortable.

Our new chaperone's sales pitch was centred on the quality of the clothes they made, the speed of their turnaround time, and low cost at which they could produce them. Every question we asked, be it about shipping, cotton sourcing or employment contracts, was answered with some variation of these three promises: quality, efficiency, and price. After all, what more would a potential buyer be interested in?

The power imbalance was genuinely shocking, and was the biggest take-away from this visit. While we had also appreciated the generosity of time at the other two factories, it was hard not to see past the difference between the Fair Trade Certified factories and the one that wasn't. The authority that Fair Trade certification provided to factory leadership meant that their focus and pitch was on doing the right thing rather than just promises of low prices and quick turnaround time.

We wanted the three things that all three companies were proposing: quality, efficiency and price, but we also knew that we had to partner with a company that cared deeply about fairness. We'd always viewed the third party fair-trade verifications (even if they were expensive to attain) as helpful to provide validation to consumers. However, now we saw why these verifications were important with buyers too. This was not just because of the impact that it had on the workforce, but because of the direct impact that it had on power distribution. It helped to give more authority in favour of the entrepreneur who had invested heavily in creating a culture of fairness. Having validation was like having some academic qualification letters after your name (MA, MBA, PhD). For people that cared, it showed them the effort that had been put in.

Factory #4 - Mandala - What Ethical Production Is All About

It was at the fourth factory that plans for collaboration became clear. Our view of what could be achieved was evolving by the hour as we learnt and digested as fast as we could. Rapid business plan development was taking place in real time. Initially, we were keen just to learn and understand the ethical business models that were being implemented. However, over the course of the trip, it became increasingly clear that there was great opportunity here, and we became hopeful of finding a business that we could partner with: a partner that went beyond a cursory, box-checking approach to fairness, and that could lead to long term collaboration.

While we had enjoyed the visits to each of the other factories, had learnt a lot, and were impressed to varying degrees with what they were offering, we weren't blown away. And then we found a true gem: Mandala Apparels.

Behind Mandala was a warm, generous woman with strong leadership and an incredibly firm handshake, Anjali Schiavina. In the 1990s, after years of living in Italy, Anjali moved back to her native India and began looking for ways to empower her local community. Her home city of Puducherry (once called Pondicherry) bears the scars of over 300 years of colonial rule by the French, Dutch, British and then the French again. Puducherry was home to well over 700,000 people, with tens of thousands trapped in the daily struggle of extreme poverty. Unlike other parts of India,

Puducherry was not a city known for having a deep apparel legacy, with the industry powerhouses being located in the larger cities with a longer history of clothing manufacturing.

Anjali was convinced that providing fairly paid jobs in clothing factories had the potential to create lasting, positive social impact. So, in 2002 she started her business in a small room with a couple of sewing machine operators and a plan to do some good in her corner of the world. By the time we met her, she was twelve years into her enterprise. What had started as a tiny seed of an idea had evolved into a Fair-Trade certified factory employing over 200 people. At the heart of Mandala was a commitment to ensuring that workers were treated ethically. For Anjali, this was about paying the workers fairly and on time, and proactively seeking opportunities to improve the quality of life of those working in her factory.

The extent of Anjali's desire to bring about social change was evident on both the micro and macro level. When one of Anjali's former employees lost all his savings in a tsunami flood, she organised money management courses for her workers to ensure that no one had to experience a situation like this ever again. She brought in experts to offer free financial management workshops. She put equal time into other education programs and brought in medical professionals to host free health workshops.

We became convinced that this was a factory with a vision of fairness at its core, to the point that Anjali did not stop caring about the welfare of her employees when they walked out the doors. This was the kind of business we wanted to support and were keen to partner with.

We were really struck by two things in particular. The first was the number of Mandala workers who were so inspired by Anjali that they had aspirations to start their own businesses. According to Maslow's hierarchy of needs, self-actualization is the highest of all our needs and is only possible when the other needs (physiological, safety, belonging, esteem) are met. We had not seen a vision this holistic and comprehensive from any of the other businesses that we visited.

We were impressed by Anjali's long-term goals. She was passionate about breaking the cycle of extreme poverty. It was so encouraging to see workers being able - and encouraged - to pursue their higher ambitions because their basic needs were fulfilled. Being treated well allowed these workers the headspace to think about their real potential. They did not need to wonder when the next paycheck would come or whether they'd have enough cash to pay rent. This sense of security allowed people to creatively and boldly hope for an even better future. A sense of the long-term is taken for granted by most of us, but those without opportunities are never able to experience this. This was a real, lasting, and profound impact, impact that could not be conveyed on a spreadsheet or glossy report. It was deeper and more personal than that.

The second thing that caught our attention was Anjali's meticulous commitment to fairness throughout the supply chain. She worked tirelessly to ensure that everyone involved in the production of her clothing was treated well, and that all raw materials were produced sustainably. She was working to ensure that all of the cotton coming into her factory was organic. This, in turn, meant that those picking the cotton in the fields were not exposed to pesticides that could cause harmful side effects. Anjali gave us an overview of modern-day cotton picking - the gruelling hard work, the reality that the best workers are those with nimble fingers, meaning child labour is often involved in the process. Anjali stressed to us how she scrutinised her supply chain to ensure that child labour was never involved.

She personally visited the plants where the cotton was woven and dyed into fabric, to ensure that her suppliers used acid-free colouring and certified chemicals. She made sure that there was a proper water management system to protect the local environment from the release of chemicals and waste. Anjali took her values even one step further. She committed to buying a minimum amount of cotton each year and to paying the cotton farmers 50% up front, before the harvest came in, before even knowing whether she would be able to sell it all. In all our research, we had yet to hear of anyone taking such immense financial risk in order to give security to farmers.

Of the four factories we visited on our four-day tour, there was no factory that even came close to Mandala. Importantly, Mandala's approach to fairness didn't mean that quality suffered. Anjali was very clear that she was running a business, not a charity. She knew that if she was going to be competitive in the marketplace, she needed to consistently produce clothes of a high standard. One thing that became clear was that we needed to find a factory partner with the capacity to produce for brands who were interested in quality, and not just fairness. And that's exactly what the Mandala factory had been able to accomplish, securing orders from multiple mainstream brands because of their high quality.

Mandala achieved that success while striving for a profound social impact. Over 70% of Anjali's workers were women. This was completely intentional. *"We primarily employ women, as the money they earn is spent on their children's education,"* said Anjali. There was no difference in her factory between what a man was paid and what a woman was paid, but Anjali regularly found a marked difference in how that money was used at home.

"There was something I started noticing," she said, *"Some of the men didn't come to work for two to three days after they took their salaries. And when I started enquiring why that was happening, I realised it was because they were spending half their salary on alcohol... If I wanted to really make a difference and see that the children got a proper education,*

then it made sense for me to start employing more women. Whatever salary they took was for their children, to ensure that their children's future was better".

Like any successful entrepreneur, Anjali was constantly innovating. Aware that many of her employees had come from the villages surrounding Puducherry to work in her factory, Anjali made a concerted effort to send work back to the villages. Many of the women in her factory travelled great distances to work in the factory. This meant that they often could only make the long journey back home to their families one or two weekends a month. Anjali had established mini-factories in houses in local villages, so that her workers didn't need to leave their children and their communities in order to find work.

So what is the price difference between clothing made at the Mandala factory versus clothing made elsewhere in India? Anjali charged just 10-15% more than other factories in order to cover the cost of paying workers fairly and on time. To put it in perspective, paying 10-15% extra is what many Westerners call a tip. Most of us give tips without a second thought. We understand that servers deserve compensation for their service. So why can't we do it for the person who made our clothes?

The scouting trip was a great success. We'd learnt an incredible amount and had established a strong potential partnership. We had found a company that we were impressed with and excited to collaborate with. In our minds, if other customers could experience even a small part of what we had just experienced, there was no way that they wouldn't buy more ethical clothing!

What was missing was visibility, a way for others to see and experience what we had seen and experienced in the factory. We believed that making clothing production more visible would be a game changer. We left India with a provisional agreement to buy clothes from Mandala. We were wildly excited.

We had also learnt a lot about ourselves and our priorities on that trip. Buying our individual wardrobes of ethically made clothing had given us the confidence that we could personally make a difference, one item at a time. This feeling was magnified on the trip, as we'd been treated, without merit, as successful entrepreneurs and potential buyers at the various factories. We now knew that we had to do more, to earn the respect that had been so freely offered. All we needed now was a customer database and a carefully planned, strategic business model. 'Simple' right? We knew it was going to be a challenge but we also knew it was what we were meant to do. **We were energised and ready. We were about to begin our ride on the rollercoaster of social entrepreneurship in the clothing sector.**

9

The launch of Visible Clothing: Initial milestones

Throughout our journey, we had discussed the need for more transparency to combat the murkiness of global fast fashion. Partly, it's the nature of the beast - a complex supply chain in a globalised economy with components coming from many different types of businesses, based in many different locations. And partly, the murkiness is intentional. Muddied water makes it harder, almost impossible, to be clear about who and where responsibility lies: pass the parcel and make sure you're not left holding it when the music stops. After the Rana Plaza building collapse, it took years for anyone to be held accountable, as multiple stakeholders denied a duty of care and eluded prosecution, passing the 'responsibility buck' to someone else.

As we embarked on the next phase of our journey, our vision was to be absolutely clear and transparent about who was making our clothes and how they were being treated all along the supply chain. And yet, it wasn't just transparency that we wanted. It was visibility that we were striving for.

Our vision was not just about seeing the supply chain clearly ourselves, but about making every link in the supply chain more clear to everyone. It was about making clear the personal and environmental impact of the manufacturing process - making the faces of those behind the clothes visible, making the costs visible, making the impact of purchasing the clothes visible. 3 visibles:

1.   **Visible people;**
2.   **Visible costs;**
3.   **Visible impact**

It was about making everything and everyone in the supply chain visible.

We had experienced this visibility when we visited factories in person, but prior to travelling to India, it had been frustratingly hard to get the level of visibility we desired from online research. And though it had been great to see the impact of ethical practices on our trip, we were frustrated that we hadn't been able to learn more about the workers' experiences and perspectives. We were convinced that the more transparency there was in how an item of clothing was made, the more the '4 Buts' could be overcome, and the more the clothing sector could be improved.

With our vision for visibility firmly in place, we set about putting our ideas into action.

Crowdfunding the Project

We pondered choices for a company name and spent hours discussing different options. We considered making up a new word, or using an acronym, and then the genius of Johnald kicked in. He reminded us to keep it simple and to remain focused on the core of what we were trying to do. Our priority was making all things related to the clothing visible, so we chose the name Visible Clothing. It seems obvious now in hindsight, but it took a couple of weeks tossing around ideas before we found the perfect name for our business.

We got our hustle on and started exploring a bunch of different ideas. We hoped to connect the people who had followed our journey of buying a new wardrobe (and the millions of other Western consumers that they represented) with the amazing, ethically-minded manufacturers that we had met in India. We believed there was an opportunity to contribute to the disruption of the clothing sector, by making things that mainstream clothing companies had purposely hidden purposely visible.

The first anniversary of the Rana Plaza building collapse seemed an appropriate date to start a crowdfunding campaign to launch the business. We'd had great feedback and responses to our blog on giving away all of our clothes. Friends and family were supportive and enthusiastic. Many people had told us that they would love to join us on the journey if only they knew how to begin. They'd also been trapped by one or more of the 'Buts' and while philosophically in agreement with us, there was no way that they were going to give away all their clothes. They needed an opportunity to kick-start their ethical clothing journey and we needed supporters to kick-start our idea. So, naturally, we set up a Kickstarter campaign.

Crowdfunding campaigns are a great way to raise relatively small amounts of money from many people, as well as to market test a new product or innovation. While we weren't testing a new product, we were keen to learn whether there was interest in supporting a new, values-driven, ethical clothing company.

The First Product

We listened to a lot of advice about how to ensure that not only would the campaign be successful in raising cash, it would also help us learn more. We were advised to select a high-margin product for the campaign. Success in selling a high-margin product would show that there was a gap in the market, proven by the fact that people were prepared to pay up for the product.

However, our goal at this stage wasn't to assess the long-term viability of a specific product or to understand profits and margins, but to learn about people's interest in the very concept of fair-trade clothing. Specifically, we wanted to see if people were as committed to it as they had claimed. It was one thing to support the idea as a concept - it was another to actually part with cash. While we were never going to make a big ask at this stage, we knew that talk was cheap and were curious as to whether people would back up their talk with tangible action.

Taking on board some advice and ignore others, in an attempt to keep it simple, we decided to go with the ageless favourite: a t-shirt. T-shirts meet many different needs for various demographics. While some loved the thin reveal-all (or almost all) fabric and figure-hugging cut, the most popular t-shirt was the standard box cut.

We were well aware of the '4 Buts' and wanted to ensure that we overcame them with our very first product. We weren't prepared to skimp on the quality of the fabric. On our trip, many conversations had been dominated by the nuances of different fabric weights and the effect of fabric weight on cost, quality, and longevity. We needed to focus on quality from day one, to ensure that the biggest 'But' that stops customers from buying ethical clothing didn't become an obstacle. We therefore chose a simple cut in high quality cotton, offered in black or white. This was partly to keep things easy for us, and partly because it illustrated how we viewed the ethics of the situation: black and white.

We wanted to source our inaugural t-shirt order from Anjali and her team at Mandala as we felt such alignment with their mission and values. As this first t-shirt was very much an exploratory product, there were so many unknowns. We weren't sure exactly what our costs would be, and so we decided to offer the shirts at an affordable price point and then work out the margins once we learnt more.

Environmental impact was critical for us, and so we went with a 100% cotton rather than a blend or a plastic infused fabric. It also had to be certified organic cotton. Additionally, we were adamant that we had to have high quality, environmentally friendly packaging. It had been sickening to see how much waste had been generated buying our new wardrobes. Due to the fact that most ethical clothes had to be bought online, there was a huge amount of single-use packaging. Walking down the high street, the waste is less obvious as the customer is at least one step removed from all those single use products. Even with a one-off delivery, the packaging waste often goes unnoticed. When we bought whole new wardrobes in one month, we became painfully aware of the amount of waste we were left holding as we unpacked all the items. Unpacking a plastic wrapped item was something that we didn't want our supporters to experience, so we sourced our packaging from a start-up compostable packaging company.

The Launch

Having participated as supporters in multiple other crowdfunding campaigns, we deliberately set a fundraising target that we knew was manageable. We were also honest with ourselves about what we had to offer: an incredibly simple product. No track record. No innovation in the product itself (the innovation was in the supply chain model). No money spent on marketing. We were going to rely on hustle and gentle pressure on our friends and families, and we hoped that a few random people we'd not yet met would share our values regarding ethical clothing.

After weeks of discussion and preparation, we felt that it was time to stop faffing and we'd learn by doing and get the project live. As we prepared to finalise the launch of the campaign, Johnald decided that he wanted to focus on different aspects of the issue. We parted ways, thankful for all the work and partnership that he had provided. It was now or never for the two of us. First thing that morning, we pushed the 'Send' button on a mass email, and the campaign was officially launched. We were off on the rollercoaster ride of learning by doing. The Visible journey had officially begun!

The campaign was a success. We were able to raise money, exceeding our targets. Prior to completing the campaign, we made the decision to take the leap and confirm the order, in line with Mandala's minimum purchase order of 1000 units per colour. Now, all we needed to do was to get the t-shirt orders delivered to each of our customers. How hard could that be? What could possibly go wrong? Unfortunately, we were about to find out just how hard it could be and experience several of the ways it could go wrong.

For such a small and simple campaign, it was surprising how many challenges we experienced. We learned early on that the only thing that we knew for sure at the start of every day, is that there would be something completely unexpected that would happen. As this was our first order and we wanted to be able to learn as much as we could from it, we deliberately didn't use a procurement, order processing, or distribution company. Instead we called in friends and family to help as we worked through the process of getting 5000 t-shirts from the factory in India to our new individual customers, most of which were based in the UK and USA.

After multiple delays and rescheduling, we were informed that 48 boxes of t-shirts had finally cleared customs and would arrive that same day. It turns out that 48 boxes is a lot! It was crazy. We'd prepared some storage space in the garage, but thought it would be smart just to dump them inside and then over the next week, methodically work through the spreadsheet and reorganise. However, the boxes were much bigger than we'd expected. We quickly moved furniture around in the storage room and created more space in an additional room. It was utter chaos. We were relieved when we finally counted 38 boxes in the main room and I was told that there were 10 in the spillover room. Boom! 48 boxes.

As the driver left, there was an eerie grin on his face. His expression reminded me of someone I'd seen before but I couldn't remember exactly who or when. His look wasn't right, but people are allowed to look however they want. It was hardly a reason to take any action or even give it a second thought. We had heaps of boxes to sort, 48 to be exact.

The next day as we finally got to grips with processing the boxes, after an initial count, recount and a third check, we confirmed that there were in fact only 47 boxes. Hunting high and low and restacking the boxes, we couldn't locate the last box. We looked over the paperwork and the number was consistent through the whole supply process. It was documented that 48 boxes had left the factory. 48 boxes had arrived in the UK. 48 boxes had cleared customs. 48 boxes had been signed out for delivery by the driver.

In our haste to take the boxes, we had even signed the paperwork stating that 48 boxes had indeed been delivered.

Either someone else had made the same mistake we had in signing for the incorrect number of boxes earlier on the journey, or someone had stolen a box of fair trade t-shirts. I then recalled what the driver's eerie grin reminded me of: it was the time I'd been pickpocketed and before I knew what had happened, a guy walked past with a grin that made me feel like I was a sucker. Ugh. We concluded that the delivery driver had likely stolen the box, but there was no proof and little that could be done. It wasn't that big a deal, but it was disheartening. 105 t-shirts were gone. As we were selling them for 15 quid each, that was over £1500. It was a painful loss, before we had even properly started the business.

We looked at filing an insurance claim but concluded that we wouldn't get very far as there was no evidence to take the claim further. The box was gone and the quicker we accepted that, the quicker we were going to be able to move on. It was a frustrating experience and we learned the hard way about paying attention to detail. More significantly, it was our first lesson in our new business: to let things go when they take a twist outside of your control. This was a critical learning that would come back to us time and again in the years to come.

The second lesson related to the range and sizing of the clothing. I'm not sure what we were thinking when we chose the range of t-shirts that we chose. Initially, we'd been intentional in keeping it simple with the colour options of black or white and a combination of fitted (female) or unfitted (unisex). But then somehow we took our eyes off the simplicity. We added colour options. Then we added different print options. And with the various different permutations of fit, colour, print and size, we were left with 55 different options! I'm no mathematical genius, but unless we were fortune tellers and had managed to accurately predict what permutations our customers were going to buy, we were making sure that we'd be left with unsold stock. Ugh.

On our very first step into operating a business, we'd gone from keeping it simple, to creating a lot of unnecessary stress, as well as ensuring we would be left with a large number of leftovers. This error resulted from our own excitement, combined with the enthusiasm that we received from people we'd asked for advice. So. Many. Opinions. While we valued the encouragement and support, the contradictions and distractions often resulted in our lives and business decisions being made more complicated.

Now, years later, it's apparent that neither of these two incidents – one in which we had only limited control and one that was 100% in our control - were not that big a deal. However, these were important lessons and themes that kept recurring. We'd learned the hard way what advice we needed to value and how we needed to own our decision-making process. Finding ways to review and check in with our own intuition, as well as to heed only the advice that drew the best out of us, was critical. We needed to find ways to access and follow our internal wisdom and to surround ourselves with people who provided insights that we did not have.

Unpacking the Crowdfunding Campaign

Once the campaign was complete, we took a moment to catch our breath and reflect on what had happened. Wanting to learn as much as we could, we reached out to the crowdfunding platform - Crowdfunder.co.uk - to give us a report with their perspective on the campaign. It was fascinating to see the data. While we weren't surprised by people's commitment levels, or by the ways that people had been referred to us, what shocked us was the rejection rate. We had run a "very successful" campaign, according to the report. It had exceeded the modest targets that we had set; there was positive feedback on the information that we shared; and we had an "exceptionally high" follow-through rate. By exceptionally high, they meant 5%! Five out of every 100 people who had seen our campaign video and who had looked at the web page actually parted with cash. The crowdfunding platform was impressed by these numbers. We were mortified.

While we expected to have a lot of questions about fair trade and what that really means, we didn't anticipate the level of detail that some potential supporters demanded. We had worked to outline our approach and philosophy, and we were really pleased with the manufacturer with whom we had chosen to partner. But we had no idea how many design and fair-trade 'experts' there were in our network who would give opinions ad nauseam. We'd spent a lot of time ensuring the quality of the product and health and safety and care for the workforce, but we were shocked by the level of scrutiny that was asked of us during the campaign. For example, we hadn't given any thought to the sustainability of the ink on the printed card that came with each shirt. Choosing 'Visible' and our claim to make our supply chain visible meant that we'd opened the door wide open to the criticism of 'armchair experts'.

Perhaps the biggest, and most unexpected, surprise was the backlash from a handful of people about the breakdown of the product's price. We had gone to great lengths to detail the costs of the product, with the goal of making the cost visible. People were upset and some even angry about the price of shipping. Shipping?! Of all the links in the supply chain, shipping was the one that we had the least control over. We had intentionally chosen the form of transportation that while slower, was both the cheapest and most environmentally friendly. Yet, we were still given a hard time and asked to justify why the workers - who were paid a fair salary - received less than the cost of the shipping. We were ready to take on the world of clothing, but it was going to be another thing to take on the whole global economic order. While we felt there would be values-alignment with a lot of customers, we realised we were going to need to be both patient and intentional in explaining our approach to being visible.

We had worked with the manufacturer to get as much information as possible about the team that had made the clothes. While they were helpful in sharing information with us, there were gaps in their answers as they clearly had never been asked to address many of these questions before. We wanted and asked for each of the t-shirts to be signed by one of the team members who made them. We had dreams of finding ways to fully trace each item of clothing all the way back to the person who stitched it. We wanted to connect with the workforce, who we very much viewed as team-mates on this journey. Unfortunately most of the initial t-shirts came back with unsigned labels. The handful that were signed were not legible. This was not a big deal and was entirely understandable, but it was disappointing.

The factory didn't have the systems in place for workers to sign t-shirts, and weren't going to incur extra costs and effort just for us, as a new, relatively smaller buyer. It was what was behind this small issue that was the bigger frustration to us. The t-shirts were fair trade and from all the due diligence that we had done, the factory appeared to be doing the right thing on multiple levels. Signing t-shirts was understandably not an important focus for them. But for us, it was important because it was about people learning about the impact that buying these t-shirts made. We realised that we needed to be able to find other ways to connect directly with the workers if we were going to get the visibility that we were hoping for.

As we looked around at the many variations of t-shirts we now had, in a huge array of colours, designs, and sizes, we realised that we were going to be left with a lot of inventory and that this inventory very quickly was going to become 'toxic'. Not literally toxic in a chemical way, but a retail expression for stale inventory that doesn't get bought. We were slowly understanding what we had brought upon ourselves. The odds were not in our favour that we would have the exact right number and combination of t-shirts for the exact customers.

We were fortunate that we were able to work with some conferences and events who were looking to bulk buy in large quantities and with wider varieties. Working with conferences was in and of itself an eye-opening and frustrating experience. Over and over again, we were disheartened by haggling over price, even for the most do-gooder of do-gooder conferences. Partly it was understandable. We were simply the t-shirt provider, clearly not at the top of the priority list at most conferences. Yet it was the dismissiveness and lack of caring about whether makers were fairly treated that shocked us. It was hard to accept that conferences that are intentionally set up to bring together people who want to change the world, use sweatshop-made clothing to promote fairness and equality! As long as t-shirts lasted the length of the conference and there weren't any uncomfortable questions being asked, then for them, it was all good. Don't ask, don't tell.

Not all of the conferences and groups were the same and there were some gems in the pack, but it happened often enough to challenge us. We were often tempted to push things by asking the event organisers how they could justify buying sweatshop clothing. But our belief in catching flies with honey rather than vinegar, and our deep desire to not guilt or shame others as we sought to bring in more people on the journey with us, made us hold back.

Even though all we were stocking at this stage were t-shirts in a handful of colours and prints, we experienced firsthand just how much waste the fashion sector creates. Because of the demands for high minimums and the inability to have production made to order, huge amounts of finished clothing products are sitting around waiting, with fingers crossed that they'd be sold. Rarely are they all sold at full retail value and therefore discounts galore are offered in hopes of liquidating stock, all due to an incredibly inefficient supply chain. We began to see enormous value in made-to-order production models, especially for smaller, ethical clothing businesses.

The Next Steps for the Business

Now that our business was launched, we began to focus on how we could deepen our impact and influence the wider clothing sector. If we were going to have an impact beyond our immediate circle, we needed more products with more originality. We would also need an online shop in order to build a brand. We wanted to find the very best and had connected with several other manufacturers in Africa and Asia who seemed like a good fit for our mission. We decided to get on the road again and meet with more clothing manufacturers to explore expanding into more product types. With the trust relationships that we had established, we were connected with a number of other potential partners.

After a number of conversations with producers and a lot of research both in person and at a desk, we decided to place an order for high quality men's dress shirts. Having heard so many opinions on the cost breakdown of the original t-shirts, we invested time and money in creating an even more detailed breakdown of the costs of the shirts that could be viewed on an app. However, the app was received with a mediocre response. Customers were curious and asking questions at the beginning of the process. But once their curiosity had been addressed, they had either decided to become our customers or not, and very rarely were they interested in getting more details. It was clear that cost breakdown wasn't the biggest obstacle that people needed to overcome.

Again with the dress shirts, we were unable to overcome the supply/demand conundrum and ended up with a lot of excess stock that would, in time, become toxic. Nonetheless, it was a great opportunity to meet exceptional entrepreneurs and learn about higher price point clothing production.

Over many months, we explored a variety of ideas that would allow our business to combat the rest of the '4 Buts'. But all of our ideas kept leading back to the biggest challenge: control, or the lack thereof. Without control, we continued to struggle to come up with a business model that would enable the connection we dreamed of between customers and clothing makers. For us to build the business that we desired to have, we needed to be able to control more of the supply chain. It wasn't enough to just be buying from those who met our values criteria. We felt that, if we could find ways to have more influence and control, we could create more positive impact and deepen the connection between the customers and the makers. We wanted to learn more, directly from the workforce, to tell their story and to educate our customer base on the impact they too could have.

We learnt the hard way when and how to share dreams and ideas, who would add value, and who would only make our lives more stressful or irritating. Negative, backward-looking people were some of the biggest energy saps. In many ways they were becoming another 'But,' discouraging others from joining the ethical-clothing movement. Surrounding ourselves with the right people was critical. This didn't mean having people that said yes to whatever crazy idea we had. When we had wise, positive people around us, we were able to see a new world of possibilities. We weren't going to try to convince those without values to suddenly get some. Rather, we hoped to provide or highlight ways for values-driven consumers to channel those values.

One of the keys to being a good entrepreneur is being wise about risks. Most times, people don't take risks when the fear of failure becomes the biggest factor in their decision making. We didn't want to look back at an opportunity that we had passed up out of fear or because we hadn't followed our intuition. For us, the risk of looking back later in life and knowing that we hadn't done what should be done was the biggest risk of all.

We often found ourselves interacting with naysayers: people who couldn't get past what they saw as unacceptable risk/reward ratios. Be it giving away our clothes or ordering 5000 t-shirts before we had all the buyers lined up, we realised that we approached risk differently to many others. We still believe that living in the 'fear-of-failure trap' keeps many would-be entrepreneurs from ever getting started.

We were convinced that there were millions of values-driven consumers sitting on the edge of the pool waiting to jump in (and we still believe this!). We were ready to take the business to the next level. We explored various business models, but the key challenge remained the lack of control. If we wanted to have a more direct impact on the sector then we needed to have more control so that we could add the most value for consumers and makers. The question was how.

10

Buying our own factory: Implementing our vision

When we received an email from an Australian company saying that they were looking to sell their business and small Indian clothing factory, we were immediately intrigued. We had not been able to visit the Eternal Creation owned factory on our previous scouting trip to India, both for logistical reasons, and because they hadn't advertised that they could make custom orders. We decided it made sense to go and have a look at it to see how it compared to the other factories that we'd previously visited. I got on a plane the very next week. Within five days I was in Dharamsala, India.

Could We Own Our Own Factory?

The idea of being able to lead our own production facility strongly appealed to us. The opportunity to have a deep direct impact on the full-time employees at the company was exciting, and felt like a challenge into which we were keen to channel our professional backgrounds and skills. However, it was the potential to be in control of an entirely visible model of production that was the biggest attraction. The goal would be not only to continue to produce for the Eternal Creation brand, hopefully developing and expanding that customer base, but to use the factory as a model to influence the wider fashion sector.

In the process of rebuilding our personal wardrobes, we had come across the Eternal Creation website and had bought clothes from them that were of great quality at a reasonable price point. We had gone back to the company to buy additional outfits for ourselves and gifts for others. We were excited about the huge volume of different designs that they had built up over 15 years, with both patterns and fabrics stored in-house and readily available for use. This established business had a solid supply chain and a loyal customer base, so investors could feel confident that there was good potential for profit and long-term viability.

As mentioned many times previously, quality had been the biggest negative aspect with other fair trade clothing brands. We knew that consistent high-quality manufacturing takes years to build, and that it is critical for creating brand loyalty and a database of repeat customers. Eternal Creation had that attention to detail that we felt we could build upon. In addition, we were impressed by their ability to have quality grading in-house, meaning that they had the capacity to produce consistently sized products - a surprisingly elusive thing in Fair Trade fashion.

Eternal Creation's physical factory location in Dharamsala had been chosen by the previous owner to achieve her mission and vision. While off the beaten track for the industry, it was set in a beautiful location and had an established network and community. We immediately had visions of bringing up-and-coming ethical clothing designers to work out of the factory. A beautiful location would surely make that decision to stay and work at the factory slightly easier.

While lots of resources were already in place, we also knew that we would need to invest a lot of time and effort to grow the business. We would need to spend time with others in the ethical clothing space and work our connections where we were based, in the UK and USA. While some work could be done virtually, face to face meetings were imperative to build trust with others in the ethical clothing sector.

After a few more factory visits, a bunch of meetings to recruit and close with investors, and extensive due diligence, we decided to take the plunge and purchase Eternal Creation's brand and factory in India. It's hard to overstate how excited we were to have our own factory and be able to work with our very own team. We felt that we had acquired some incredible assets, both in terms of physical fabrics, designs and machines, as well as an incredibly talented workforce. Over the next few months, we made multiple more in-country visits and worked with lawyers in four jurisdictions to acquire the company assets. A very long and tiring story short, we eventually got the deal done. Our next chapter had begun.

Listening and Learning

While we weren't able to move to India full-time, we were committed to going as often as we could, to being flexible, and to spending time at the factory in person as much as the need arose. In the first year of owning the factory, I spent so much time in India sometimes it felt like I had moved there. Sometimes trips were scheduled many months in advance and other times it was at 24 hours notice.

We expected the learning curve to be a steep one, but we were pleasantly surprised by how many things worked out well. On the flip-side, we were shocked by the multitude of challenges that we didn't anticipate and which often blindsided us. It was a complex combination of feelings whenever we were with the team. On the one hand, we were energised and motivated whenever we spent time with them, be it virtually or in person. They were a wonderful group and we saw huge potential in them. Every time we spent time together, it strengthened our commitment to growing the business to have an even more positive impact on their lives.

Simultaneously, it was intimidating to be reminded of the huge responsibility that we carried. On a daily basis, we were responsible for decisions that had a direct impact on the employees, their families, and extended families. Being mindful both of those who had put their trust in us, and of our vision to have an influence well beyond our own company, we woke up each day with a high level of excitement and very often finished the day with an equally high level of stress.

Investors often talk about risk/rewards ratios from their financial perspective, but for entrepreneurs, the question of risk is more personal. Entrepreneurs are the kind of people who choose to double the number of hours they work, exponentially increasing the amount of stress that they have in their lives, while working indefinitely for low pay. The risk/reward ratio is insane as compared to most traditional investments. Yes, there are substantial financial rewards and incredible career satisfaction for entrepreneurs who are successful and who manage to make a substantial cash exit, but 99% of social entrepreneurs are never going to have a payoff that comes close to compensating for the relentless work and stress that they have taken on. Stories of huge financial success in this field are few and far between. Entrepreneurs are sometimes labelled as crazy, and often ridiculed for not knowing what they are doing. Social-entrepreneurs are viewed as even more crazy for believing that they can make money and change the world at the same time. Yet, these are the people who are pioneering a new path, who are bringing about much needed innovation.

Our plan for the first six months was to simply focus on the day-to-day operations of the factory. Our approach was to listen and evaluate so we could gain a better understanding of how the operations were really working in practice and not make snap decisions. We had a little runway financially with the investment capital that we had raised, along with the revenues already coming into the business from sales. We were confident that we could take the time to undertake a thorough review of the business from the inside. Therefore we didn't initially invest in a lot of team training. Instead we wanted to see what and how the staff were doing and make assessments without the team feeling the need to perform.

We also wanted to listen, embracing our core value of empathy, as we started creating our company culture. Some of our approach was methodical, carefully planned out and would have met the criteria outlined by consultants or pontificators. But the biggest successes in this initial period were when we were open minded, opportunistic, and intuitively embracing of opportunities when they arose.

The factory team was initially composed of 35 full-time members. Unusual in the clothing sector, the majority were men. A number of tailors were migrant workers who had come to town specifically to work at the factory while their families remained hundreds of miles away. Most of the tailors had extensive experience in cutting and sewing and we could see that they had truly exceptional skills. All of the more experienced tailors on our team were men.

The management team had been in place for a number of years and there were long standing working relationships among the various team members. The vast majority of the team warmed to us immediately, and their attitude towards us coming in as new owners was welcoming and hospitable. Saanvi would always greet us with an incredible smile and her positivity was a great start to the work day. Aarna focused on making sure that we always had a thoughtfully made cup of chai. Each time that we saw Durga, she was keen to teach us a new word in her mother tongue, one of the 300 languages in India.

Other team members were more wary. Amir would occasionally break out in a huge grin, but could also be awkward and downright stubborn. His initial somewhat aggressive behaviour took us a long time to figure out and remained confusing months later. Ishaan was one of the least skilled workers on the team, but clearly was used to getting his own way and feeling like he was the boss. Vihaan just had a generally unhappy disposition and life always seemed to be a struggle.

We were drinking from a fire hose and learning by the day, sometimes even by the minute!

From the numbers that we had seen, everyone was being paid fairly. The factory structure had been set up principally to produce orders for the Eternal Creation online brand. A variety of different rooms had been rented on the property, and there was a fairly well organised and effective production system in place. It was a unique set-up and fit well for a customised production model. The more vocal members of the team told us they were happy and that it was a great place to be working. But we also saw opportunities for growth, both financially and in terms of impact. In the first three months as we transitioned into establishing ourselves as new owners, we began to see a multitude of opportunities for deeper values alignment.

Apparently a newborn child learns over 50% of their life learnings in the first three months of life. That steep learning curve was similar for us, and in no way more so than in regards to the team. As we spent more time meeting and working with them, time and again over the next few months, we sensed different approaches and feelings towards us. These reactions were occasionally expressed verbally, but more often non-verbally. The majority continued to be kind and welcoming, while unfortunately, a handful progressed from an initial, understandably nervous reaction to being downright obstinate. As with many new relationships, boundaries were pushed to see 'what can I get away with'. However, it was incredible how a handful of bad apples not only took up a lot of our time and energy but also gradually influenced the rest of the apple cart.

We realised early on that that it was going to be critical to be focused on implementing the work culture that we wanted to create. We had to find ways to ensure that troublemakers were not allowed to cause unnecessary disruption. We had to motivate those who had the potential to be great collaborators, but who for a variety of reasons were holding back on giving their best for the team. For example, it slowly became clear to us why Amir, who had been so hard to get a smile from, was such a hard one to win over. Amir was extremely reluctant to share his expertise or teach others how to be more effective in their jobs. He was incredibly talented and had clearly worked hard at his craft over the years to get to the level that he was. When there was a specific skill or technique that he was uniquely able to do, Amir held on to it for dear life and refused to collaborate. At times, he would even try to sabotage things to ensure that his status remained unchanged.

As we reflected on this problem, we sought first to understand the feelings and motivations that Amir and a few others had. Why were he and a handful of others so reluctant to collaborate? Why did they have such a strong belief that life was a zero-sum game and there could only be one winner and many losers? It became clear that this reluctance to be collaborative was connected to the cycles of extreme poverty that had defined their lives for so long. Job security and unique skills were of astronomical value in a low social-economic setting, with limited opportunities to advance. If that meant refusing to teach others how to realign a sewing machine in a specific way, or refusing to collaborate with a sampling tailor on how to follow a more intricate pattern design, then that's what workers like Amir were prepared to do.

Once we were able to understand the root causes that were blocking a collaborative approach, we were able to make changes and adjustments so that team members were rewarded for helping and collaborating. They began to see that their job security increased, rather than decreased, the more they acted as team players.

Amir was a good guy who deeply cared about his family. Unfortunately, with the life circumstances that he had been born into, he felt that he had to act in his own best interests at the expense of others. In one case, Amir deliberately tried to engage me in a power struggle by disrupting the working day. He took other workers away from their assigned jobs and tried to call a team meeting. I flirted with the idea of guilting and shaming him, but that would not have aligned with my values. Instead, I tried to act with patience, logic and grace. Amir was trying to push my buttons and bring out my competitive instincts to drag me into a confrontation, but his plan couldn't be allowed to work. I knew that no matter how stressful or difficult the situation was, I needed to confront it head on and prioritise our value that no-one is bigger than the team

We needed to constantly remain clear on what our values were and stay committed to a plan to live into those values. But what were those values and how were they going to be implemented on a daily basis?

11

Core values: The heart of every social enterprise

Values have been at the heart of our journey. From the start of our initial involvement into the ethical clothing sector, living into our values was our primary motivator and so they were intentionally at the core of how we wanted to run the factory and build our business. This chapter outlines the values we decided upon, and in the next section, we share how we tried to live into those values as business owners and leaders.

Our initial vision statement was: *"Imagine a world where everyone in the clothing sector is treated fairly".* We had this statement printed on some t-shirts left over from our crowdfunding campaign. As it was a long and rather awkwardly worded statement, a casual look was not sufficient to take in the full meaning of the sentence. This was either marketing genius or stupidity, depending on who we were talking to! After a sneaky, or more often, not so sneaky second glance, people's responses proved to be fascinating, resulting in good conversations and strong sentiments of agreement. However, when we were wearing the t-shirt at clothing-related events, or at social entrepreneurship events, the response was often a lot more critical or sceptical. *"How could that ever happen?"*; *"What does that really mean?"*; or the downright rude *"What that t-shirt is trying to promote is not possible"*. Unsolicited opinions such as these were ungraciously shared with us more than once.

We came to accept that our vision statement was too wordy, a little clunky, and that the goal it expressed was too lofty. We were realistic about how massive the clothing sector was, and we didn't expect that we personally could change the entire sector. We were, however, convinced that the sector had to be changed. We believed that our kids' generation would look at the fast fashion industry that our generation so easily tolerated and be horrified at the injustice. We weren't proposing sitting on feelings of guilt and shame, but instead channelling those feelings into solutions and hoping to be catalytic in bringing about wider change.

And so we worked to create a more succinct mission statement that would focus on what *we* could do as a company. A useful exercise that we undertook was to reduce our mission statement down to seven words or less forcing us to focus on our most basic values and goal: **'Treating team-members fairly; influencing the clothing sector'** (notice that we put team-members together to get it to be 7 words or less!).

While the wording continued to evolve, the values themselves did not. We always came back to the original '3 Visibles' that we'd used in the crowdfunding campaign: People, Costs and Impact. We used the 3 Visibles to outline our go-to-market and marketing plan and our values, and the conviction to live them out more fully, that were going to underwrite everything that we set out to do. As soon as we acquired the factory, our first priority was identifying the company's core values and articulate how we were going to connect them to the 3 Visibles.

As we prepared to launch Visible Clothing, we'd spent a lot of time discussing and reflecting on our personal core values. We considered how we wanted to conduct ourselves as individual leaders, and then in turn what we aspired to be as an organisation. We regularly came back to these values over the course of our journey, whether to make sure that Andy's grandmother would approve of us not telling a lie, or trying to act in accordance with Andy's mother's advice to *"Be kind to everyone regardless of who they are."*

For us, identifying core values wasn't a dry values exercise that was just done on some wannabe corporate retreat with an emotionally detached consultant and team members that didn't care about the topic (does that sound like we'd had that personal experience before?!). Defining values was critical as they were at the very centre of who we were and wanted to be. The challenge was to incorporate the values into a wider company culture and to ensure that as far as possible, we were practising what we preached.

The Golden Rule

The backbone of most established religions and philosophies is "Do unto others as you would have them do unto you," commonly referred to as the Golden Rule. Variations of the Golden Rule have influenced the creation and implementation of cultural norms and structures across various societies over the centuries. The basis of the rule is that compassion and generosity are extended beyond immediate families and friends, continuing to neighbours and others in the community. It means we must have respect for others, including those outside our immediate circle. As we undertook this journey into the world of ethical clothing, it was the critical application of the Golden Rule that underlaid everything we were trying to achieve.

While there were clear regulations and laws being broken at Rana Plaza, it was the persistent lack of application of the Golden Rule in the clothing sector at large that left such an oppressive and cruel state of affairs. The lack of adherence to the Golden Rule allowed a situation like Rana Plaza to exist, and allowed for wanton disregard of human life and dignity to be prevalent across the whole industry. If those holding power in the clothing sector reflected on the Golden Rule and chose to apply it more directly to their work, the fundamentals of the sector would immediately and drastically change.

The Golden Rule was the foundational and foremost of our core values, informing all of the other values. If we were going to have the impact that we wanted to have, we needed to consistently and proactively try to put ourselves in other people's positions and understand their perception of reality.

Value #1 - Empathy

Despite so much historical oppression in the industry, there was arguably more empathy in the clothing sector in the past than there is today. That empathy existed, in a large part, because of the geographical proximity of the factories to consumers, as well as the fact that the labourers looked more like us. Clothes makers, tailors, seamstresses and other clothing sector workers may have come from a different social class to the consumer, and there may have been stark differences in their culture, but until relatively recently, they lived in the same geographical place and there was a clear and undeniable connection. Neighbours, or those living nearby in another town or on the other side of the tracks, might be working in horrible conditions and being paid a pittance of what they were worth for their labour, but they were still in our physical vicinity.

Sadly, we have been historically and culturally conditioned to be less concerned about those in far off lands: those who were part of historical empires, or those who are less educated, or viewed as being less 'developed' than us. However, it has always been a cultural given that we had to, in some small way, take care of those living nearest to us, regardless of their lot in life. The responsibilities of the upstairs elites in Downton Abbey included the obligation to ensure that the downstairs workers were taken care of via employment. The economically privileged ensured that the workers in the village earned enough of a wage to survive and to keep working for the elites, even if nothing else was offered to them. It might have been 100% self-serving, but there was a clear moral (even if not legal) obligation to ensure that those who were less fortunate (or who were intended to occupy a certain space in society) had at least the most basic of resources – food, healthcare, mental well-being – to maintain or sustain that place. It was far from perfect, there were horrific inequalities, but there was a stronger connection due to the closer physical proximity.

By channelling even just a little more empathy to act with compassion, the wealthy elites could become heroes – be it Cadbury in the 1850s providing decent housing for his factory workers, or Rowntree in the 1900s establishing schools so that their workers' families could be educated. Business leaders were often viewed as being a part of bringing about social reformation when they acknowledged and addressed social injustice. While fuelling their business growth, empathy was an understood social interaction that was morally required. While the societal structure meant that everyone 'knew their place,' it would have been morally reprehensible to not have some degree of empathy for the people whom they could literally see sitting on their doorstep.

Both mass manufacturing of clothes locally and increased globalisation dramatically altered that. The 'race to the bottom' and the creation of sweatshops on a global scale fundamentally changed the way that we interacted with the people who work in clothing manufacturing. As the world has become smaller and smaller, in terms of being able to more easily connect and cross geographical boundaries, so our moral responsibilities have expanded, whether we acknowledge it or not. We are now concerned about wars that don't directly involve us, in previously 'far flung lands'. We now have more morality questions about what is the right or wrong thing to do for example by intervening (or not) in genocides based upon complex multi-generational challenges, of which we previously had minimal understanding. It's hard to ignore these social justice issues as they are live and present in our living room televisions, and even more directly through the internet and social media, in ways that were unimaginable for our grandparents.

The interconnectivity caused by globalisation has grown more and more powerful, to the point that we no longer even need to take the steps to go into the living room. Now we can get the constant 24/7 feed on our handheld devices, or even on our watches. Governments can try to hide this interconnectivity by changing passport colours or threatening to build walls, but the reality is that we are more interconnected now than ever.

Yet, the clothing sector has managed to remain in an intentional bubble. To a large extent, the industry pretends to detach itself from the shrinking effect of globalisation all around. In fact, while most other cross-border boundaries have gotten smaller and easier to penetrate, the clothing industry has become more impenetrable. While barriers have broken down in other sectors – tea, coffee, even bananas - the obstacles to fair-trade in the fashion sector have remained strong.

Steps that have been taken with the expressed intention of bringing more transparency to the supply chain have been consistently manipulated or abused. In 1995, the World Trade Organisation (WTO) instituted the requirement that the place of manufacture needed to be clearer and transparently shown on a product. This was when the "Made in X" phenomenon started. While this regulation gives us the perception of knowing where clothing has come from, it does very little to increase accountability in the supply chain. Instead, it has been used to fuel nationalism and state pride, clouding over the reality that over 95% of the production of clothing takes place overseas, often in the most marginalised communities and almost always hidden from view.

One of the questions that we kept coming back to was: Who has the moral responsibility for how workers in the clothing sectors are treated? Whom does the responsibility ultimately lie with? And perhaps more importantly, who should have that moral responsibility?

It is easy to feel empathy when we see on our TV screens those who have been unfairly impacted by a tragedy or natural disaster. While we might not have experienced that ourselves, we feel an obligation to help or to give, or at least to think about it. We feel a sense of responsibility to bring about change, because we know that it could somehow have been us if we had just been a bit less fortunate or if we had been in the wrong place at the wrong time. Disasters bring about empathetic emotions that can lead to thoughts such as 'There but for the grace of God go I'. The easier it is for us to imagine that we could have been in that situation, the easier it is for us to see the complete unfairness and tragedy of an unjust situation.

And yet, when it comes to more complex or systemic inequalities, confusion about what we can do makes the situation more complicated. Instead of an immediate knee jerk reaction of compassion, we remain distanced and our brains come up with justifications and complications that prevent an empathetic response. Even if one was to try to address these complex challenges, there are often factors ingrained in our society that have intentionally created a level of complexity that makes it impossible to fully comprehend the problem, let alone a solution. It's hard to know where to begin chipping away at the enormous iceberg of complex social injustices.

Once awakened to a social injustice, we're left with two choices. We either try to step up and confront the issue, or we add it to the long list of 'would like to be involved if I had more knowledge, time or energy'. Movements such as #MeToo or Black Lives Matter cause us to make a choice as to what stance we want to take. Knowing that they are happening and still saying that we are not taking a stance is still taking a stance. Yes, there are complexities and ambiguity in all social justice issues and no social justice movement is perfect, but we can find clarity when we decide how our legacy is going to be defined by the stance that we do or do not take. We have the choice as to what our actions are going to be, or what excuse and reasoning we are or are not going to hide behind. History is watching.

In light of our growing understanding of the crucial importance of empathy to bring about positive change in the world, it was easy to agree that empathy was at the core of what we wanted to do and achieve as a company. We had seen other companies and organisations that seemed, over time, to lose focus on their mission. Whether it was the lack of focus on their mission that had led to a reduction in empathy, or the reduction in empathy that had led to a lack of focus on their mission, we couldn't be sure. It was, however, sad and disappointing to interact with companies and entrepreneurs who had lost their heart.

We desperately didn't want to be those people, so we set up a structure to ensure direct conversations and honest feedback between ourselves and others whose opinions we valued. Over the first few months of owning the factory we had many moments of utter frustration and disbelief, but the support of others who we trusted and who got it, encouraged us. We were reminded time and again of the mission that we were trying to achieve.

The value of empathy was great in theory but became even more impactful in practice. Once we were able to spend more time with the team, and had the incredible privilege of being invited into their homes, sharing more intimately the journey of life with them, it was impossible not to feel more and more understanding and empathy for the life of a garment worker. On rare occasions, we were pleasantly surprised at the relative wealth a handful of team members had. However, the majority of the time we were distressed by the level of extreme poverty that they were experiencing. Many times, we were deeply touched and inspired by the level of community and hospitality that they shared with us.

Like empathy, karma was a regular topic of conversation in our work. Partly this was a result of having a factory based in India, with its deep spiritual history. Partly, it was the diversity of worldviews and religions on our team. Most significantly, it was the fact that we were in a business whose mission was beyond any one individual. Whether individuals believed in karma or had views on ultimate accountability or eternal judgement or not, there was a consistent belief that individuals had a responsibility beyond what was in the near-term and the immediate view. While most of those whom we worked with took the mission very seriously, we were shocked and disappointed by the number of people from across different races, religions and beliefs who would discuss the importance of empathy and karma and then act with a complete disregard for others. We had to keep reminding ourselves: Actions speak louder than words.

Value #2 - Integrity

Acting with integrity was critically important to us as individuals as well as to us as leaders of the organisation. We weren't trying to play games; we were trying to do the right thing, be that in the way that we interacted with our own team, suppliers, customers, or other stakeholders. The focus was on trying to be consistent, honest and truthful in all situations, and on many levels, that made it easier for us because the rules of the game were always clear. At least clear on our end, that is.

It sometimes made our work astronomically harder when others were not playing by those same rules. Even in the fair trade, do-gooder world, there are some people trying to take advantage of others who are willing to exploit the fact that others are seeking to act altruistically. We would regularly say, as part of our collaborative decision-making process, "Well, we can't lie. Therefore, we have to say...". We tried to be wise and strategic in how we shared challenges, problems or mistakes, but we'd remind ourselves that if we were trying to act with integrity, we had to tell the truth, even if that would make our lives more difficult in the near term. While our commitment to integrity resulted in many difficult conversations that we would have preferred to have avoided, it did take a huge amount of pressure off us. We had no choice or other way out. Come what may, we were trying to act in the right way even if that wasn't the most comfortable way!

That's not to say we were pure or perfect in any sense. Far from it. We made mistakes aplenty and let ourselves and others down many times. We manipulated and played by different rules that weren't part of the game that we committed to. On some occasions, we realised that if we had information that was not apparent at the time, we would have approached things differently. Sometimes, it was even more simple than that. We just weren't the best of ourselves, and we made mistakes. We messed up. However, the more we were able to surround ourselves with those who lived into the value of integrity in whatever form that was, the more inspired we would be to be the best of us.

Value #3 - Quality

Empathy and integrity were values that were part of our personal social entrepreneurship journey but not specific to ethical clothing. So many of the barriers that we had experienced while rebooting our wardrobes could be summed up with one word: quality. We believed that many more customers would get on board the ethical clothing train if they felt confident that they could consistently get excellent quality clothing.

We had been amazed at how much work went into ensuring there was high quality with our crowdfunding campaign when all we had made were some very simple t-shirts. We made the choice at the beginning that we weren't going to compromise on quality even if that meant that the process took longer than we wanted, and because of the extra costs involved, left us with lower profit margins. It was clear early on that quality was something that we could not and would not bend on. Right from the beginning, we insisted on good quality fabrics and good quality production. We even implemented our own additional level of quality control after we received the t-shirts. We were rewarded by multiple comments from our supporters expressing their surprise at the quality of the t-shirts.

We were aware that ethical clothing customers had been stung in the past with poorly cut clothes or awkwardly fitting designs, so we wanted to make sure that Visible was known for high quality products. We also wanted to be known for high quality customer service. While it was understandable that small, cash-strapped, ethical clothing brands didn't always have the resources for consistently producing high quality products and offering excellent customer service, we felt that it was imperative if we were to have a voice and influence in the sector.

We also strived to maintain high quality in our marketing and communications. Over the course of the journey, we tried a variety of different ways to communicate with customers. Some worked, some didn't. It was hard to create effective genuine communication of our story in the way that we felt was consistent with our company. The line between authentic, honest communication and poverty tourism was something we had to carefully navigate. We wanted to convey the challenges of extreme poverty while not eliciting pity, and without disregarding the strength and dignity of the workers. 'Poverty tourism' had shocked us in the past where those most marginalised had their lives exploited to give Western consumers or donors a heart wrenching story.

We explored and committed to other values along the way, but empathy, integrity and quality were the cornerstones of what we aspired to be. That said, none of these values could be successfully implemented without our fourth and final value...

Value #4 - Fun

With all the intensity of the work, and doing all we could to achieve our mission and adhere to our values, we had to remind ourselves that we also needed to enjoy life and that having fun in the present moment was good. Even more than good, critical. In our experience, a fun work environment was a more productive work environment. We set out to be a well-rounded company where the team enjoyed going to work every day. Again and again, we were reminded that the most critical thing for the team in at the factory was the guarantee of being paid so that they could meet their many financial obligations. Once that level of security was established, then fun was a value that was much more attainable.

Upon reflection, as we dealt with all the stresses and strains of launching the business, the importance that we put on the other core values at the expense of our fourth value was perhaps too much at times; we too regularly lost sight of fun. Ironically, as two people who strive to be non-trouble-making class clowns, this was the hardest value for us. As we recognized and incorporated the value of fun, it took the pressure off and allowed us the freedom to enjoy the unique experience of starting a business. When we were able to take a step back, we were able to laugh at the insanity of start-up businesses and giggle at some of the ridiculous experiences that we were having.

Intentionally investing time and effort in the team's approach to having fun helped to increase productivity and focus. There were parties at cultural festivals, with hours-long party games, incredible feasts, the world's loudest DJs and learning Bollywood dance moves until the early hours. The parties and feasts into the night meant that the next day, when the team came together, they were more collaborative and willing to embrace innovative approaches. It wasn't just about the occasion, but about the memories that were made together that led in time to greater efficiencies. Over time, the trust that was developed through having fun together increased the team members' respect for each other and also for us.

We were pleased with the work that we put into creating our core values and, we spent hours working with our team, engaging in various exercises, group discussions and team building exercises to try to ensure that everyone was aligned. Yet it was our own individual actions that were the key and were ultimately the only thing we could control. It was how we handled immense stress and challenges that most reflected our core values. And, whilst it was great to feel confident that we had a thought-through, rational, heartfelt set of core values, we had no idea just how important and challenging it was going to be to stick to them on the rollercoaster journey that lay ahead.

When the rubber meets the road, who do we want to be? Our story is not an idealised one, sugar coated to make us look like social-entrepreneurial gurus. Instead its an attempt at honest and real reflections on us and our company, sharing a few of the many lessons that we learned along the way as we leaned in to living out our values through the 3 visibles.

12

Visible #1 - People: Building our social enterprise DNA

The first year of running the factory and business was by far the busiest time of our lives. Every aspect of the work - from ordering raw materials, designing new products, managing production, managing people, conflict resolution, hiring and firing, sales, shipping, and customer service - was an opportunity to live into our values. Sometimes we fell short of our ideals, but we never stopped striving to live up to the values we had chosen. We worked tirelessly to inspire the team to do likewise. This was our whole purpose of buying the factory: to do things differently, to make things visible, and to be driven by values and not just by profit.

Over the previous few years, we had done a lot of work evaluating over 100 different companies in the ethical clothing space. In addition to deciding whether we wanted to partner with them or buy their products, we had assessed these businesses to understand what we perceived to be their company DNA and their commitment to fairness. Now we were focused on building and creating our own company DNA in line with the 3 visibles: people, costs, impact.

Our first 'visible' was people. Now that we were in control of our own production facility, we wanted to get to know our team better, given that our vision was all about making the workers' lives and perspectives visible in a respectful way. We were keen through visible business storytelling to increase the connection between our production team and our customers. When we started Visible, we had dreamed of having a company owned by all of the stakeholders (including the clothing makers), with the goal of overcoming traditional, power-based divides. Over the many months that we had spent preparing to acquire the factory, we explored various ways of raising investment and creating an employee ownership model, which seemed like the clearest and most equitable model. Employee ownership was the example that was suggested by many theorists and we'd heard a lot of talks and pontifications about such models being the holy grail in the social impact space. We'd also reviewed several models that included employee stock options that would allow all our team to earn equity in the company.

However, as we quickly discovered, owning a share in the company or having stock options was not a priority for the workers at the factory. After talking and listening to the team, it became clear that stock ownership options were low down, at best, on their life goals. For those who had evaluated the possibility, it was viewed as overly complicated and unnecessarily burdensome. They were smart team members who knew their worth. They wanted to be able to come to work, to work diligently, and apply the skills that they had worked hard to develop; all while being treated with respect and being paid equitably. What they didn't want was unnecessary stress. Their number one goal was job security and safety, they wanted regular income and bonuses based on their success.

They wished to be treated fairly, relative to their peers. Given that an employee ownership model was legally difficult to create, and was not wanted by the team, we determined instead to implement what the team expressed that they did want; to share in the success and profit of the company through regular, good salaries and equitable bonuses. This required us to undertake a thorough audit and salary review. We planned to use this process to bring the team together as we continued to listen and adapt, based on what we heard and leaned.

In the first six months of owning the factory, the more that we listened, the more we understood that we needed to be discerning regarding who it was that we were listening to. It wasn't just about hearing from the powerful and vocal team members. We needed to hear from people across the organisation and to ask for opinions and feedback in a way that all team members would be comfortable sharing. We faced a huge challenge in getting feedback from many team members and overcoming cultural barriers to honest communication. This was based both on being different nationalities, but more significantly due to drastically different cultures and life expectations, based on gender, wealth, power, and privilege. Some voices would be intentionally silenced during team discussions. Both the fundamentals and nuances of viewpoints would get diluted when views were shared with us through middle management or local language translators.

While we listened to many sales pitches for various software packages and apps to collect team members feedback, we found that the most effective way was to go old-school. Using good old fashioned pen and paper, we set up an anonymous suggestion box. It was such a simple idea and yet turned out to be incredibly effective. It gave a platform for team members to communicate with us directly, rather than through an intermediary who might have their own agenda, or require them to use a technology that they didn't trust. Even those whose formal education levels were not that advanced were able to find friends outside the company who could write comments and feedback for them.

We were mindful of the vulnerability with which comments were shared, and respectful of the trust that had been created, allowing people to feel like they could talk and write honestly. We were also aware of the classic suggestion box shenanigans wherein we got the same message, literally word for word, five different times but in slightly different handwriting! Obviously, we didn't just change course and incorporate every suggestion, and it was far from a perfect system, but for the most part, it worked well. It was useful for us as leaders to hear everyone's input. The more shy and previously voiceless team members finally felt like they had a voice. Their suggestions were heard and often sparked changes, which led in turn to more people speaking up. As we responded with a similar vulnerability to that which had been shared with us, more trust was created.

However, not all the feedback was what we had expected. At times we were shocked by what we learned. Reports came in that cut to the core of what we were trying to create, and were a painful wake-up call. Suspicions that we had harboured since doing our due diligence to acquire the business were confirmed. For example, as we reviewed changes to quality control, we heard on repeated occasions, "What do you expect? Of course the quality is bad. She's a woman. Women can't sew". Tragically, we didn't hear this only from men. Hearing such misogynistic comments was deeply distressing. We realised that we had a big problem around gender equality, and that what we were hearing directly was probably only the tip of the iceberg.

We decided that we needed to confront the gender issue head on. We were aware of cultural expectations and norms, but nonetheless, it was critical to speak and act in line with our values. It was blatantly clear that this wasn't right. Additionally, we felt that it wouldn't be respectful to the team to accept such misogynistic behaviour. We knew that the long-term effect of not addressing these attitudes would lead to more serious problems down the line.

Similarly, when we discovered evidence of products missing from the company, we had to take immediate action to redefine and realign our company culture. We weren't exactly sure how to go about this, and couldn't see a win-win scenario and felt that we needed more time to get all of our ducks in a row before taking action. However, the more we gave into our weaknesses of avoidance and procrastination, the more stress we experienced.

Being fair trade does not mean being taken advantage of. So, after multiple attempts to resolve these problems through dialogue, we decided to change the management structure and let people go who were not aligned with our values. We knew that it would need to be a complete overhaul and reorganisation and that it would have repercussions across the whole company. However, while it was hard to do, time consuming, and very frustrating, the long term impacts turned out to be incredibly positive. By changing the management, we were able to make massive headway on pivoting the culture to be in line with the company values. We were committed to building a culture based on values that were both visible to the customers and also behind the scenes within our own team.

In hindsight, we wished that we had been more decisive and proactive even earlier. I'd love to say that this was a lesson learnt just once, but unfortunately, it was something that we experienced too many times on the journey. When things weren't taken care of directly in the first place, with topics being swept under the rug or just ignored, very rarely did problems miraculously disappear. It was a fine balance between giving ourselves more time to think and process, and taking swift, decisive actions.

Creating a 'Do the Right Thing' Culture

In many cases, we were forced to take a step back and review what was appropriately culturally, versus an oppressive tradition that should not be tolerated in the workplace. We weren't trying to create some sort of utopia, but we wanted to develop a new cross-cultural way of life within the factory.

The experience of giving away all of our clothes had affected much more than the way we looked: it had also profoundly changed the heart of who we were. It changed how we wanted to be in the world. It changed how we looked at other consumer decisions, and even more significantly, it forced us to think deeply about culture. What was the reality of the culture that we were born into? What aspects of our culture did we feel confident would withstand scrutiny under the lens of history? What was currently acceptable and what would be acceptable as the moral universe continued its long arc towards justice?

We sought to nurture a 'do the right thing culture' within the company. Of course, we too often fell short of that culture in our own actions. However, we did our best to live into this ideal in our daily work interactions and were intentional in the way we worked with the team. For example, to us, making everything visible meant that we had an open door policy. We took that to the point of giving out our personal phone numbers so that anyone from the team could reach out to us directly whenever they needed.

While people are inherently selfish to various degrees and are motivated by a combination of optimism and fear, we believe that most of the time, most people are trying to do the right thing. The vast majority of people who we encountered working in the clothing sector had similar life goals: almost all were motivated by the fundamental desire to care for their families and for those in their close community. There will always be some who can't think beyond themselves, a tiny, yet often vocal handful who are out for themselves alone, heedless of the consequences for others around them. But realised pretty quickly that this tiny minority could easily take up the majority of our time and energy and be a distraction to others who were more aligned with our mission. We learned to deal with these troublemakers in various ways and, honestly, with varying levels of effectiveness.

On the flip side, we encountered many incredible people who had a sincere desire to care for those beyond their closest community. These inspiring individuals envisioned a community beyond those they personally knew, positively impacting the whole society. They embraced a 'Do the right thing culture' and could be relied upon to model that and share with others.

No-one is Bigger Than the Team

The complexity of cultural and generational challenges was ever present in the workplace. It was absolutely heartbreaking to hear stories of infanticide and forced adoptions that were experienced by our staff members and their extended families due to financial challenges and burdens that came with being born into poverty. When Rohan stayed late one day, we knew that something was clearly wrong. We also knew that we weren't going to get a straight and direct answer immediately and would need to ensure that we were patient. It felt like we were talking for a couple of hours before we eventually got to the heart of the issue. Female infanticide. The more that Rohan talked, the clearer it became that his whole family was being disrupted due to gender inequality and cultural expectations.

These cultural expectations were a whole new paradigm to us. To this day, it's hard to fully understand all that was going on. We had never spoken with anyone about forced adoptions, and our only exposure to infanticide was from textbooks that we had read in the classroom. It's not appropriate to share more details here as these very personal stories are not ours to tell, but there were multiple occasions that we felt completely and utterly out of our depth. Coming back to our core values, we had to expand our empathic abilities more than ever before to try to understand lives that were vastly different from our own.

Sometimes we were left feeling powerless as we were unable to have any clear impact with the team members that we had grown to care about. It was painful not to be able to fix a problem, or even come close to offering any kind of solution. Yet, that was the reality of running a social-enterprise seeking to impact extreme poverty. It was like the teaching we had both received when becoming TESL (Teaching English as a Second Language) teachers two decades earlier. We were taught to focus on students who knew the answers and were keen to learn, but weren't as vocal as others. To find ways to create cohesion among the various members of the group. To bring out those on the edge but who were hungry to do more. We focused on being proactive in ensuring that everyone was set up for success and felt part of a bigger team.

It was an ongoing challenge to fully comprehend the thought process of someone trying to break free from the trap of extreme poverty. Countless books have been written on theories and approaches to breaking generational cycles of poverty. We hadn't read all the books, but we had reviewed more than our fair share, and we were fortunate to have learned from leading academic thinkers on poverty. However, it was only when we were able to spend time listening to and empathising with people on the team, that we could truly comprehend such a different world view and reality of life.

For every team member like Rohan who we were able to listen to and empathise with, there were team members like Ishaan who weren't interested in becoming part of a team. It was hard, almost impossible to work with Ishaan, and with a couple of other trouble-makers like him who weren't willing to collaborate. The ongoing, deeply rooted and regularly recurring impact of extreme poverty in our team member's lives and spirits forced us to listen and adjust as we tried to establish the work culture that we wanted to create. Some of the challenges required us to have more empathy. Some required us to just be strong and honest in staying true to our mission.

The phrase that we stated most regularly with the staff was that 'No-one is bigger than the team'. Working effectively with people is obviously essential for a fair-trade company. As in all workplaces, there were egos that had to be managed, and consistently we needed to remind the team members that the company, and more specifically the vision, was bigger than any one individual. As we tried to make everything visible, it meant that we had to make things internally visible within the company. It was a gamble, with some risks, but we felt that it was necessary. Being visible about what everyone was paid changed the power dynamics within the company overnight. Being honest and open with the team meant that confusing and hurtful games previously played out behind the scenes were now being played out in the open. One of the most contentious issues in the ethical clothing sector is the issue of pay structures.

After we had made substantial changes to our management team, we undertook a couple of internal reviews. After listening to the team and speaking with others in the ethical clothing sector, we decided to make a fundamental and impactful change: altering our pay structure from piece-rate to salaries. The piece-rate structure favoured the more skilled tailors who were able to make more complicated pieces of clothing completely by themselves. They were paid more for making high priced items, but this obviously didn't favour the less skilled tailors who were unable to make the better items and who, without a specific training program, were never going to be able to make the more complicated, and therefore better-paying pieces.

The piece rate system also didn't favour our sales team, as the tail was wagging the dog. The tailors wanted to focus on certain pieces of clothing that they could be paid more money for regardless of what that meant for sales price or for margins for us as a company. This dynamic hindered our approach, especially when trying to create a positive, 'No person is bigger than the team' work culture. We wanted the team ethos to extend across the whole workforce, not only to improve the efficiency of our production, but also to improve morale and collaborative interaction. Rather than finger pointing at others when things went wrong, over time, people learned that the more that they pulled together as a unit, the fewer mistakes were made. The stronger the teamwork, the better the quality and the greater the likelihood of everyone receiving more pay, bonuses and increased wages. When we removed the piece rate system, we still closely monitored the data, accessing how productive each tailor was being in relation to their experience. If their performance dropped, then they were called into a collegial meeting with management to find out what had happened.

Firing

When we came into the factory one Monday morning to find that Darsh, one of our strongest tailors who rarely made a mistake, had decided to quit, we felt annoyance as well as disappointment. It was different from when Arjun, one of our cutters, had decided to quit. Arjun quitting had been brewing for a while and he had been increasingly disruptive for the team. It was an emotional relief when Arjun was finally gone and, honestly, it felt fantastic to come into the factory knowing that we weren't going to have to deal with his belligerence.

However, when Darsh quit, we had the opposite emotional reaction. He'd been a courteous and reliable teammate. We had enjoyed working with him. His quality of work was fantastic. However, it was annoying to hear him arrogantly proclaiming the fact that he was more competent than all of his colleagues. While it was objectively true, his consistent demand that he was worthy of a substantial pay increase on a number of occasions (something that we disagreed with) was tiring and not helpful for the team dynamics. Regardless of how much we valued Darash's work, we weren't going to play secretive games behind closed doors or openly disrupt our whole pay structure.

We knew that we had to be willing to let people go when the company mission and values didn't fit their priorities, trusting in our values more than short-term ease, and allowing people to go with strength, but also with grace. We therefore accepted Darsh's resignation without rancour. As we explained the situation to the rest of the team, we reminded them of our commitment to the team culture that we were trying to create. We immediately had to make some changes to the production structure so that negative effects of Darsh's departure were minimised and the team could feel positively about the changes even being a valuable colleague down. Although it was annoying, overall we felt that the situation had worked out as well as it could and that next week we worked hard to bring the team back together.

It was somewhat surprising that just a week later, Darsh came by our flat one evening and asked for his job back. Whether it was the delayed realisation of what he had given up, or recognising the reality that he wasn't as indispensable as he had previously thought; either way it presented an initial dilemma as we had appreciated his work quality so much. Even though we'd missed his productive work outputs the week that he had been gone, after a little discussion we concluded it wasn't much of a dilemma at all. We believed in second chances and had given many more opportunities to various team members, however, this time we needed to stay focused on our mission and the belief that 'no one is bigger than the team' was the priority. We moved forward without Darsh, but with a more cohesive team.

We learned early on that we had to respond to threats and ultimatums with compassion but also with strength. When team members came in saying that they deserved to be paid more, we always tried to remain open minded and consider their case on its merits. More often than not, we felt that the case was without merit and so would try and explain that as rationally and fairly as possible, keeping in mind the background of many of the workers and understanding just how much of a big deal this was. It was absolutely natural and understandable that they wanted to increase their earnings and make use of every advantage they could. As we shared with the example of Darsh, there were situations when we weren't able to find a solution that was in line with an individual's wishes while also being fair to the rest of the team. When we didn't feel the case had merit, we would try and explain that directly and tactfully. But nonetheless, our decisions were sometimes met with threatening and aggressive responses, which initially surprised us. At other times there were oversights on our part that we appreciated being brought to our attention. We would look for ways to reallocate resources and responsibilities to better reflect the work that was being done and bring greater efficiency to the wider team.

Hiring

Our approach was a blend of strategic insights that would have made MBA consultants ecstatic. Other times it would have (and did) make the social-entrepreneur wannabes go crazy. Sometimes, it was formulaic and strategic in how we hired a new team member, following a standard interview and reference collecting process. Sometimes it was a lot more random. For example, we met Steph Kent, who would later become our creative designer, on the way to visiting the factory. We had already spent time evaluating what we felt we needed in terms of design direction and had started to roll out our strategic plan when I randomly met her on the plane. After learning more about Steph's background and reviewing her work, we knew that our intuition was correct, and it was going to create a long term trust-based working relationship. Steph moved to the factory and spent time developing some incredible collections as well as some important personal connections with the team. Looking back, the most important thing about Steph wasn't just her incredible design abilities, but how much she cared about her colleagues. There was a deep values alignment, more than we could have written up on a job description. Not only was she a very gifted designer, she also played a critical role in helping to develop and implement our social and environmental impact approach.

Asking Steph to join the team as a result of a plane conversation was one of the most spontaneous and yet strategic decisions that we made.

We also experienced frustration finding good candidates for important hires. While founders are motivated by a deep desire to create a business and take on something new, motivations and understanding risk among the people who want to join an entrepreneur on the journey can be very different. Joiners often come from very different starting points than Founders. At the core, start-ups are a rollercoaster ride and there are a multitude of different approaches and techniques to riding roller coasters! Some join in after much consideration, some are more impulsive and will join the ride just to see where it goes. Very few are prepared to drive the lead car while the track is still being laid and no safety checks have been completed.

After we got over this frustration, it became clear to us that there were two ways we could find the right kind of people for the team: hiring from outside or hiring from within. Over the years we ended up doing a combination of the two approaches. Hiring from the outside had the positive effect of bringing in new fresh ideas and ensuring that the new person was outside of the immediate cliques and problems of nepotism. On the flip side, it was a big venture to hire from the unknown where we didn't have the benefit of history and personal connection.

After the initial experience of working with people who we didn't know, we decided to change our approach and work with people we did know. Hiring from within had multiple benefits. While it meant working with people who were perhaps not the strongest candidates on paper, it also meant that we were working with people whom we knew – the good and the bad. We could make a more accurate judgement on whether there was a values alignment with that individual. While there was arguably more work and training to be done with insiders who were not necessarily the most qualified, working with people whom we trusted turned out to be more than worth the investment in training. While time consuming, working off a trust relationship aligned on company cultural and values provided to incredibly effective.

Positivity and Constructive Criticism

We knew other social enterprises who either chose, or more typically were forced, to have a formalised board very early on in their business. Time and time again, we'd seen this model stifle innovation and sap away motivation from founders. It was one thing to meet a legal requirement as outlined in the company bylaws, or to work with a wise and supportive Board of Directors. It was another thing to see entrepreneurs who felt a sense of existential despair and dread every time they were due to have a board meeting! Having people on the board who had not actually built businesses or who weren't fully aligned on the social mission could be excruciating to social entrepreneurs. It can be both a massive time suck and a distraction that hinders start-up entrepreneurs from achieving their potential. Conversely, we had also seen horror stories of entrepreneurs who refused to take any advice at all. They were arrogant in their personal beliefs or moral superiority that they weren't able to hear common sense from anyone.

We tried to strike the right balance: to bake in accountability both legally and morally to the business; as well as utilising resources from which we could gain encouragement, positivity and constructive criticism. More important to us than impressive resumes on paper was having advisors whom we trusted and who were reliable, committed to the vision, and most of all, supportive and kind. Lots of people were all too willing to give their opinions! It was harder to find advisors with motivations that were aligned with ours and a willingness to partner and learn alongside us on the journey. We appreciated those investors and collaborators who challenged us to be the best of who we could be. They reminded us to keep coming back to our mission. And sometimes we just needed to talk to someone who could lift our spirits, saying, "You can do it", with an uplifting positivity, even if that felt very far from the current reality that we were experiencing. Again and again, it came back to values and collaborating and partnering with people who we were aligned with.

Control What You Can Control

While our belief in what we were trying to do remained strong, our appetite for, and confidence in our ability to overcome generations of cultural structures diminished over time. At the start, while trying to be semi-realistic, we had incredibly strong beliefs in just how much we could achieve. Over the course of managing the factory, we continued to bring about changes in the way that the team functioned, but it became clear that many issues that we idealistically wanted to confront and resolve were not going to be changed in months, or even years. These were culture clashes that we were going to have to face indefinitely or at least over multiple generations. Truly understanding the cultural complexities was fundamental, as we assessed what we could realistically overcome, or what was so wound up in longstanding cultural norms that we would never overcome.

'Control what you can control' was a statement that we turned to regularly and that provided comfort at times when we saw and heard about horrific cultural oppressions. Infanticide, abusive marriages and intentional restrictions of choices were just some of the surprises that we wanted to influence but couldn't control.

Some of the other situations that we had to address were absurd and completely beyond our control. For example, on May 20th 2016, the Indian federal government announced that they were going to change their currency. Overnight. Over the next few weeks tens of millions of people were scrambling in all manner of ways to change their now old money to the new money. While this was a show of government strength which successfully cut down on money laundering and other corrupt activities, it was the most marginalised who were the most negatively impacted. Workers were left waiting in line at the bank for hours and there was on-going disruption for weeks. Additionally, we had a team of interns from a UK university, working on a project. They were left in a foreign country, with 'cash' in their hands that no longer had any value. We were left renegotiating timelines and deadlines as half the team was out of the office at any point of time. It was bizarre and, like everyone else, we were completely unprepared.

The ABC of Business – Always Be Closing

Tenacity and grit were necessary for dealing with uncomfortable issues and behaviours that were in contradiction to our mission. The ability to be tenacious and consistently 'gritty' is at the core of a social-enterprise's DNA. However, sometimes that grit would get lost or overwhelmed with the urgent and exhausting needs of the day. For example exercising that same grit and determination to follow up with every sales lead was an even bigger challenge. We had to continually motivate ourselves to pursue sales opportunities and generate new sales leads. Selling was critical in order to live into our goal of of providing consistent and fairly paid employment to our team.

The fear of rejection was not the dominating factor for our slower-than-hoped-for sales growth. Instead, it was the annoyance of having to make the same points over and over, constantly trying to convince people to do the values-driven thing. It became an ex-hausting time suck. Much of the time, it felt like we were swimming upstream.

Selling and closing with customers who had expressed interest in learning more about our products regularly dropped down our priority list. It was easy to become insular as we dealt and focused on the day to day highs and lows of running the business. When we did devote time to sales, it was difficult to decide upon the best time and expense allocation as the clear pathway to success. The only certain thing that the data across the sector showed us, was that a high attrition rate among customers was a given.

We quickly concluded that making sales and consistently following up on leads needed to be a much larger part of our daily lives and strategy. Sales calls had to be prioritised, regardless of the perceived emergencies of the day. Consistent recurring revenue was the name of the game, and keeping the pressure up to get to a close meant regularly and consistently working the pipeline of revenue opportunities. This was the only way we would be able to honour our commitment to the workers to provide consistent and fair pay.

Leadership Boundaries and Inaction

We had to learn to identify and honour our boundaries. As British men, this was a particular challenge! Short- term pushes and working long and odd hours were fine from time to time, but they easily became the norm rather than the exception, and caused too many negative long-term consequences across multiple areas of our lives. The times that the company was most effective was when we were firing on all cylinders with the mental capacity and capability to make wise decisions in the best interests of all the team members. We needed to ensure that we were in a healthy place mentally, regardless of the drama and challenges of the day, week or month.

Those times that we just sat on issues that we knew needed to be addressed proved to be an energy and time vortex for everyone involved. It happened too often, and even when we should have known better. Sometimes an issue was truly impossible to solve as the parties that we were dealing with were ultimately not interested in reaching a resolution. Gaslighting and circular reasoning forced us to take a step back on more than one occasion. We also had to be vigilant about perfectionism. 'Done' was often better than 'perfect', as long as it was in alignment with our values.

At times we avoided conversations that we felt were too difficult, which is an unfortunate aspect of our culture as Brits. Feelings of disappointment and shame about failure, or more specifically, the anticipated shame that would come with the consequences of our failures, meant that we sometimes made difficult matters much worse by not being proactive and direct. Sometimes we had to navigate through times where we knew people would be disappointed, either because we had made mistakes, or because we saw things were just not going to work out as we had hoped. As we learned more about our personalities and accepted honest and helpful feedback, we were able to get better and become more effective as leaders.

13

Fair trade: Values business in practice

The World Fair Trade Organisation (WFTO), outlines the 10 principles of fair trade:

1. Create Opportunities for Eco Disadvantaged Producers
2. Transparency and Accountability
3. Fair Trading Practices
4. Payment of a Fair Price
5. Ensuring no Child Labour and Forced Labour
6. Commitment to Non-Discrimination, Gender Equality, Freedom of Association
7. Ensuring Good Working Conditions
8. Providing Capacity Building
9. Promoting Fair Trade
10. Respect for the Environment

As we entered the second year of ownership, after such an intense period of learning and listening, we were finally starting to feel like we had a grasp and an understanding of the operations side of the business. We had set up structures that were in line with our values, adding and subtracting members of the management and staff and continued to make progress to create a (mostly) smooth running and collaborative team. There were challenges which we were still addressing, but we were seeing positive progress, as we applied a fair trade philosophy in line with our core values.

Fair Trade Saves Lives - Literally

Some of the principles listed above were more pertinent than others, and some required more work to actualize. Although challenging to apply these principles, over the next few years, we were able to see just how impactful a values-driven business could be. The culture that we were able to create and directly influence meant that the team literally directly saved a life.

Bridget was an integral part of the team from the moment that we had acquired the business. She truly embodied the fair trade ethos. She was amazing at customer service and taking care of our client needs, but even more critical was just how much she cared about her colleagues at the factory. She treated everyone with kindness, and made a point of being attentive and inclusive to those on the margins. Bridget brought things to our attention that we would have otherwise missed. "The thing is Andy...." became her opening catchphrase, a prelude to challenging us on yet another topic. She was a straight shooter. We all knew where we stood with Bridget, yet her forthrightness was tempered with sensitivity and compassion. We leaned on her insights and wisdom a lot and along with our customers, we appreciated her honesty and direct feedback.

One morning in April 2017, we woke up to a gazillion WhatsApp messages. Some were from team members who were in regular communication with us. Others were from phone numbers that we didn't recognize. We knew that Bridget had been sick for a few days, but we were not prepared to hear the news that she had taken a rapid and drastic turn for the worse. Bridget had a support network outside of work, but it was her colleagues at the factory who really stepped up and, as we found out weeks later, literally saved her life.

Initially, Bridget was taken to a local doctor who minimised the seriousness of her condition. A day later, she was taken to a local hospital where they realised the seriousness of her condition, but didn't have the resources or abilities to provide a solution. As Bridget shared in a blog post a few months later, if not for the persistence of her colleagues - who weren't prepared to settle for the medical response and who and made the decision to move her to a much more expensive hospital a few hours away - she would not have survived the crisis. Without having the ability to afford it, her teammates took it upon themselves to take her there anyway.

This critical decision that was a key factor in saving Bridget's life was followed by more valuable decisions that were a reflection of the fairness and the 'do the right thing' culture that Bridget had been so instrumental in helping to create. Her colleagues took time off work outside of their allotted hours of leave, even with impending deadlines. They made wise decisions about her healthcare, with the belief that we would stand behind them. They trusted their intuition and acted decisively, using their own best judgement, rather than waiting for someone else to take the responsibility and the risk. They didn't fear they would lose their jobs because of the work time they missed taking care of Bridget. Possessing the comfort that the company leadership would support them gave them the confidence and freedom to think creatively about the best solutions.

Shortly after this episode, once we knew that Bridget's health had been taken care of, it was time for the team to receive their annual bonus, a full month's wages for each team member. They unanimously agreed that they wanted to pool their well-deserved and well-earned bonuses to contribute to Bridget's healthcare and recovery costs. It was a truly wonderful and heartwarming story providing an affirming and fantastic example of the life- changing impact that fair trade can have.

The trust that had been built among all of us played a large part in giving everyone the confidence and the wherewithal to do the right thing. Rather than feeling powerless, defensive and fearful for their jobs, the team accurately predicted that if they were 'doing the right thing,' then their jobs would remain secure. Team members felt secure and empowered enough to take the days off that they needed to support Bridget, as well as to make a collective cash advance to meet her medical costs. This concrete example of the positive impact of our work exceeded our hopes and expectations. It was inspiring for us to see and encouraged us to keep going, to do more, and to share these opportunities more widely. After all the struggles of the initial learning period, it was a moment of enormous encouragement and hope.

Our Late Payment Dilemma

About three years into owning the factory, we found ourselves in a dire predicament: we were not going to make payroll on time. We had always prided ourselves on the fact that, since our inception, we had remained faithful to our commitment to pay workers fully and on time. Now, we were facing the painful reality that we were going to fail to meet that goal, a goal that we considered somewhat sacred.

As hellbent as we were in making sure that everyone was paid consistently, there was sometimes a massive scramble at month's end. Sometimes that meant putting in our own money to ensure that wire transfers would arrive on time. Frequently, it meant that we ourselves weren't paid as the bank balance was just too low. After a few months of this far from sustainable situation, we were suddenly faced with a new challenge: a couple of customers were late paying us for their large purchase orders.

For a while, we had been stressing to the team the importance of getting these orders out on time. There had been frustration over the previous few months as we made changes to improve efficiency. The tension had been caused by a lot of unforced errors, and it was clear that we were not all pulling in the same direction as a team. We focused on getting to the root of the problems, and had been spending an exorbitant amount of time addressing obvious and easily correctable issues. Meanwhile, orders had been delayed and internal quality had slipped. As a result we were not able to chase our receivables (money owed to us), and had been on the back foot with buyers due to minor, but persistent, quality control issues. This had all started to happen since we switched from paying piece rate to paying a consistent salary. It wasn't the only reason for the current challenges but it was definitely a major factor. Incentives were not aligned and 'do the right thing culture' seemed to only be going one way.

For several months, it had been a scramble to meet payroll. We had always found ways to overcome it, by raising more capital or by invoices finally being paid just in time. We had also made changes to our cash flow management system to compensate for the crazy time delays for invoice payments. Unfortunately, this time, our options and our luck seemed to have run out.

The feeling of dread as we prepared to break the news to the team was sickening. We had hustled and we knew that money was going to be wired shortly, but it wasn't going to make it on time to cover the immediate payroll needs. Working in start-ups before, we had experienced various kinds of intentional delays in payment: checks that were 'in the mail' rather than wired to allow a few more days for the buyer to get the funds into their account, emails with invoice attachments that had to be resent as they claimed not to have received it the first time, taking advantage of a ridiculously long payment schedule, and straight up obnoxious bullying and lying.

In this instance, we weren't in a position to put more of our own cash in, and didn't have time to dip further into the company's financial reserves. We didn't want to have to lay off team members as they all had stated that job security was critically important to them. In any case, every team member would be needed to produce the incoming orders we had committed for the next quarter.

There was no choice but to have the difficult conversation. As we ummed and ahhed trying to avoid the conversation and the uncomfortable truth that it represented, we once again went back to our core values for insight. We decided to act with empathy and integrity and be as direct and transparent as possible. When we first took over the factory, we had been met with some antagonistic and aggressive behaviour at team meetings. We'd let go of many of the instigators and learned who were the most logical, influential and wise amongst the team, especially those who were not in management positions. We'd come to rely on them to provide a balance within the team.

Telling the team that we were not meeting payroll on time was the antithesis of everything that we had set out to achieve. Not only did we feel bad that we had let everyone down, but we were fearful as to what it would mean for the team culture. Would the team splinter and people leave to look after their own self interests? Would the handful of bad apples who we had worked with to channel their feistiness manage to mobilise the others against us?

Unfortunately, neither of us were able to be at the factory in person for the conversation. On a video call with the entire team, we were honest, direct and clear about why we were in this payroll predicament. We took full responsibility for our own mistakes. We referred back to conversations over the preceding weeks warning the team that this was a possibility. It wasn't a case of "We told you so," but an explanation of consequences arising from decisions that we had all made collectively. There was a lot of back and forth as we opened the meeting up for questions. People were obviously disappointed and upset and made those feelings very clear. Some team members told us in no uncertain terms just how bad this was going to be for them. We acknowledged their distress and agreed to have another call in a few days to update everyone on the situation. We ended the call feeling absolutely awful. We were mortified. Not just because of the situation that we were in, but also because one of the problems that is systemic in the clothing sector is not paying factory workers on time. We were now part of that same problem that we detested.

Over the next few days we continued to hustle away with the outstanding invoices. If at least one of them would land, we could get the team paid. Meanwhile, we waited nervously to hear and see what the repercussions within the team were going to be. We resigned ourselves to dealing with the consequences, however negative.

But, over the next few days, we were shocked by what transpired. The next week was one of the most productive that we had on record. Projects that we had been trying to get done for months were suddenly miraculously completed. Orders that seemed to have disappeared into the abyss were found and sent out on time. Things that we had been pushing for months to make happen, suddenly happened. Conflicts that had been exhausting and apparently unresolvable were amicably resolved.

The number of shipments sent out that next week was more than the whole of the previous month combined. It wasn't a miraculous act of God. It was that team members - now directly feeling the pressure of the late payroll - had become less self-focused and started to pull together. Individuals realised that all the interpersonal and production issues that we had been talking about truly impacted the company bottom line. Team members correctly concluded that the gravy train of being paid regularly, regardless of productivity and sales, had come to an end. As one of our team members told us *"We didn't realise that when you said you didn't have any money that you actually didn't have any money, until you didn't pay us on time. We trusted you as you always paid us on time, so when you didn't, we knew that what you had been saying about the delayed orders was true"*.

We achieved more to bring about changes in those few days than we had in the last few months...And eventually, everyone got paid what they were owed, and we moved forward and managed to avoid finding ourselves in that situation again. As we reflected on this story in the following weeks, we had mixed feelings about what the lessons were. Should we not have paid the workers on time before so that we could 'teach them a lesson'? (We quickly dismissed this idea). Should we have hustled harder to get ourselves into more debt with a short-term loan so that we could pay them on time and not cross that sacred line? Was it all about the trust that we had built and the authenticity of our pain in telling them that we would not be paying them on time?

This is a story that we are not particularly proud of, and it garners different reactions from people depending on their approach to management and fair trade. While we would never have deliberately played games and deployed the tactic of putting the team under unnecessary pressure, the experience was an eye opener about how to incentivize the group to achieve our shared mission. Everyone learned a lot from this uncomfortable season. Over the following months, we continued to see the positive impact, and frequently referred back to it in order to reinforce the need for collaborative team behaviour.

Power, Privilege, Inclusivity and Gender

The disposable nature of semi-skilled garment workers across the clothing sector means that the power dynamic is massively skewed in favour of the check writer, be that the large brand intentionally delaying on a purchase order to maximise their cash flow, or the factory owner who deliberately holds back on payment as a sick power play.

We realised that a lot of education was needed among our team on what fair trade meant in practice, rather than just being an additional add-on represented by a certificate on the wall. We put real life fair trade and visible policies in place (such as a whistleblower policy) and created a revamped HR manual that outlined views on equality. We also spent time establishing an inclusive fair-trade committee. We intentionally wanted to hear and empower voices from across the company. We asked employees from a variety of backgrounds whose voices we appreciated and views we valued to be part of the initial committee. Our intention was to be inclusive across gender, religious, economic and cultural barriers.

The fair-trade committee was set up to gather opinions from across the organisation and to provide an opportunity for team members to be able to voice their opinions, safely and reliably. The committee also made recommendations about how feedback could be incorporated into practice. We asked six people from across the organisation and from different departments to join the committee. The commonality was that they were powerful voices that needed to be heard. We didn't want to just tick the box and have a committee to make ourselves look good. We wanted to create a structure for hearing from the teammates that we most needed to hear from.

It took some time for the team to get used to these initiatives, but with the trust that was established through the committee and through regular check-ins, team members gradually gained the confidence to speak their minds. Showing that we had heard feedback and directly and visibly addressing various issues showed our willingness to respond.

We were committed from the beginning to the ongoing work of addressing gender inequality, but we were naive in underestimating how hard and pernicious this would be to address. Gender-lens investing has been growing in popularity in the impact investing sector over the past few years, and there are now more and more mainstream conversations about gender and diversity. In the same way that we had had to learn to channel our theoretical beliefs with the practical realities of creating Visible, so we had to adjust our views on diversity as once again we were in the process of learning by doing.

Yet again, beyond the box ticking, maintaining the culture and DNA of fairness within the company was paramount. Having women on boards, committees, or in management positions is all well and good, but if women's voices are not respected and therefore not powerful, then these efforts at gender diversity can become detrimental. For us, it was about finding ways for women to be more powerful, and more importantly, for finding ways for women to exercise the power that they already had. Ensuring that the loudest or the most aggressive voice (either male or female) wasn't the only voice that was heard was crucial (and often challenging).

We were ambitious in what we attempted to do. We also had to regularly remind ourselves that there were limits to what we could achieve in this area. Much as we wanted to make instantaneous change, centuries of gender oppression were not going to be overcome by our personal influence. Still, it was heartbreaking to hear stories from women on our team who, simply as a result of their gender, had missed out on significant opportunities in life or had suffered extreme oppression.

We acted decisively and strongly when we heard, saw and experienced incidences of behaviours that were not in line with our core values. However, it was a consistent uphill battle, and we knew that we had to be proactively inclusive rather than reactionary. We viewed issues of gender related empowerment and opportunities with a multi-level approach philosophical belief, management approach and day-to-day interaction.

Philosophical belief: We could control and change our philosophical approach, but it was a very different challenge to influence other people's philosophies. As we matured as company owners, we saw more and more how prevalent gender inequality was. Sadly, the first time that we were told about an incident of female infanticide, was not the last and our minds were blown open on multiple occasions. We were reminded on a regular basis of just how much power we had been entrusted with and the responsibility we had to use our privilege wisely. We spoke with leaders who we respected who were working on gender equality, and we slowed down to listen and reflect on what our own team was telling us. We adjusted our beliefs when we saw successes and celebrated all the wins, both big and small. However, most of the wins remained small in our minds. Supporting women in dealing with the uphill battle to overcome day-to-day challenges that came with a lack of power was hard work for us, and we were men. We had a responsibility to be open minded and keep learning more so that we could be better leaders.

Management approach: As the amount that we learnt increased, we repeatedly updated and adjusted the company HR manual to reflect our deepening understanding of the challenges women faced in the workplace and in the world. Recruiting, hiring, and training practices were adjusted and tweaked to apply the values of best management practices, and we tried to adjust our expectations with increased flexibility. We changed our hiring process to ensure that not only were more women being asked to apply for open positions, but that the interview process was set up to encourage more inclusivity. We developed partnerships with other organisations who had more experience with women's recruitment. It was a slow and difficult process, so we collaborated with additional groups who were specifically looking for employment opportunities for their existing team of women to be able to continue working together. We adjusted our internal management process to ensure that there were more opportunities and training for women leaders to increase their responsibilities within our company.

We realised early on that finding senior staff members who we could hire, and who were aligned with our values, was going to be really hard. One factor was the fact that the factory was located in a geographical area outside of the traditional clothing sectors, so there was a smaller pool of candidates overall. But the larger issue was the abusive practices that were endemic in the clothing manufacturing sector as a whole, causing those who had abilities and options to go elsewhere and work in other sectors. The result is a small number of women leaders in management positions in the clothing sector. The data shows just how important it is for everyone to have role models and leaders that we as individuals can look up to and feel an affinity simply because we look like them. However, it was equally important for the team to have management that they felt represented them and their views. In some cases, the strongest advocates were actually men. Sometimes it was a lot more important to have management who cared about equality, regardless of their own gender.

Day-to-day interaction: Theory and principles written in guidebooks may guide managers, but they are only as useful as how they are applied to real life settings. A turning point for us was when we tried to get objective data to make equitable decisions. As part of our salary review process, we undertook some objective testing of the team's effectiveness and looked at the facts that the data provided. It was eye opening. As we went through the performance of each person on the team, a clear pattern emerged. Not only was each woman being given a low score for each of the objective criteria, but after each performance review of a woman, there was either a sigh or a dismissive shake of the head by the manager giving the review.

As we reflected that night and reviewed our communication over the last month, the duplicitous nature of what was going on became apparent. It was clear that not only were the female members of the team being critiqued more harshly, but the work allocation and expectations to meet goals and target timelines was unfairly skewed to ensure they could never excel. Female members of the team were intentionally being set up for failure. It was shocking to see such blatant prejudice and a structure that was so unfair within a fair trade company! Unconscious bias (only a little), conscious bias (a lot), and confirmation bias were all at play. Over the next few days, we sought to understand and to observe more patterns of such behaviour before taking action.

It was hard to know what exactly was being said in private management meetings, and the comments in public meetings were often only revealing in the sense of how much silence or whispering they generated. This was a massive turning point for us personally, and a pivotal moment in our careers. Again, being mindful and aware of our own personal roles was critical. Not standing by while women were subtly (or not so subtly) slighted, having a zero tolerance for derogatory attitudes, and being proactive in trying to set up women for success, were ways that we had to step up and live into our values. It was the right thing to do, but after most interactions, we didn't feel like we were directly able to achieve very much. However, we had to keep trying, given that overcoming inequality and injustice were at the core of what we were trying to do. Along the journey, we often remembered the 'little' wins and the fact that however frustrated we were, individuals were still being positively impacted.

Eesha, an experienced tailor on the team, was excited to finally be pregnant again and overjoyed that she would have a guaranteed job to return to after her maternity leave. As we got to know Eesha and shared stories with her about my own wife's pregnancies, she opened to me about how important it was for her to be able to have this child. She expressed her joy in having financial security and job stability so she could enjoy her pregnancy, free from some of the stress of poverty. She was also keen to take on as much additional work as she could, to earn overtime pay in preparation for the extra expenses she was about to incur. While we were able to share in the joy of Eesha being pregnant, we were struck by how sad it was that she had been forced to have an eight-year gap between her children, simply due to financial constraints.

Kiara, a less experienced tailor on the team, explained to me that at a young age she had been forced to drop out of school and find work to support herself and her family. She had never had the opportunity to be trained, or been allowed to develop the skills necessary to increase her income. While she was literate, she had never been given the level of education that she dreamed of for her daughter. Kiara's primary motivation for becoming a better tailor was to increase her income so that her daughter would not have to go down the same road in life. The school fees match that we offered not only gave Kiara an additional incentive to educate her daughter, but also provided a little extra validation. She felt encouraged that the goal of her daughter completing a secondary school education was attainable.

As we started working with other brands and organisations, several different designers (the majority of them women) would come to visit and work at the factory. One of our initial hopes, which was to some degree realised, was that we could use this opportunity to inspire some of the women on the team about how they too could achieve exciting new goals.

We offered other activities that gave opportunities for deeper conversation. After a number of team meetings to discuss gender bias and equality, we decided to host a company cook-off. Each team member had to bring their favourite dish to compete with the rest of the team. The only criteria for each dish was that it had to have a connection to an important woman in their lives. We got to hear a number of stories about mothers, wives, sisters and daughters while we all shared in a great feast. Even though some of the conversation was rich and deep, I'm not sure how much of a lasting impact it had on the team, but it sure had an incredible impact on me. Firstly, as the team-appointed chief culinary judge, I had to try at least a mouthful of each dish. Truly amazing, wonderful food, but by the end of the meal I was stuffed!

Secondly, and more importantly, it was eye opening just how much further on the journey we all needed to go. So many biases and cultural disparities that ranged from just plain stupid to absolutely heartbreaking. The arc of moral universe is very long and needs to be incredibly bendy if it is to end in justice. However, history has shown us that it does indeed bend towards justice. We needed to double down and make both the big and small decisions in order to play our part in bringing that justice into more of our daily reality.

At the first opportunity that we had to recruit a new manager for the factory, we took the opportunity to recruit a women leader with an inclusive approach. We had seen directly that just having women in positions of leadership was not enough to overcome systemic gender imbalances. In fact, having women in leadership who didn't have an inclusive approach could actually be more detrimental to creating an inclusive work environment. From the first interview that we had with Saanvi, we came to understand that there were multiple layers of biases on our team, both conscious and unconscious, explicit and implicit - that needed to be addressed. Thankfully, Saanvi was incredibly gifted and qualified to take on this challenge. Her management approach was a powerful combination of strength and grace. On a consistent basis, she provided us with encouragement that fair trade principles made sense and did work. We were motivated to do more and make profound impact.

14

Visible #2 - Impact: Meaningful more than measurable

Our second 'visible', impact, was focused on the direct positive social impact that happened when customers bought in line with their values. We were convinced that if customers were aware of the positive social impact that buying ethical clothing could have in the world, it would make it much easier and more compelling for them to make a more conscious choice.

Alongside thousands of other social enterprises, we were focused on having the relevant measurements in place to assess our progress towards the United Nations Sustainable Development Goals (SDGs). Our primary impact was directly on the lives of our employees. Our view on impact evolved over the time that we owned and operated the factory. Based on the reality of the situation, we adjusted and tried to improve our approach. The more that we have worked with people in extreme poverty, the more we've understood its complexity and just how little we know. Additionally, the impact that we felt we could realistically achieve altered as we adjusted and tweaked our business model. On the individual level, we were excited about multiple other direct and personal impacts that we were able to be a part of creating. Employees who had previous experiences of working in the wider oppressive clothing sector would share their horror stories with us that were truly shocking. It felt great to regularly hear that our factory was a safe workspace, emotionally as well as physically, in contrast to the majority of clothing companies.

What Are the 'Best' Impact Metrics?

Initially we wanted to have a focus that was focused on employee retention. Based on what we had learned from social impact measurement experts, we knew there was a desire for uniformity in measuring social impact across the sector. We learnt that converting subjective personal impact into objective numbers can be difficult, if not impossible. We were focused more on creating opportunities for positive impact than on finding ways to measure it. While it's great when employers provide a positive place to work that gives employees a desire to stay working, this metric can have a detrimental impact when it becomes the primary definition of success. For us, the fundamental mindset shift took place when we had one of our greatest impact successes. The story of Diya turned our standard impact answer on its head, even if it counted against us in traditional social impact measurement standards.

Diya was a skilled tailor who was always keen to learn more and increase her abilities. While she wasn't the fastest or the most efficient, her focus and reliability was impressive. She also had a constant desire to improve and to give her best. We invested time and effort in helping Diya to bring the best out of the skills that she had, many of which had been developed at a much later age than many of her male peers. Diya was a fantastic team player. She was diligent about helping her colleagues to succeed, even if that was at the expense of her own efficiency. She insisted on being seated next to Devansh, who while reliable and fast as a tailor, was constantly playing catch-up on any new designs or production processes. Diya was adamant that she would work closely with Devansh as much as she was able. She ensured that whenever there was a call for new scissors or for machine needles to be changed, Devansh was not left behind. Indeed, this team-forward attitude exemplified by Diya and a number of others, mostly women, was one of the main reasons that we moved the model from paying piece rate to paying salaries. The fastest tailors weren't necessarily the best tailors for the team's success as a whole. Overall team performance was more important than individual success.

As we continued to deepen our trust with Diya and as she got used to the regularity of a consistent, guaranteed income, she opened up about the challenges of her home life. She shared about her abusive husband and her longing for a fresh start in a new community, away from the place where she felt trapped and helpless. Both she and we knew that she had to get out of town and rebuild elsewhere as soon as she was legally free to do so. We continued to focus on opportunities for Diya to improve her competencies and learn more skills. Eventually, Diya gave her notice and went off to explore the new opportunities that she had been dreaming of but previously unable to attain. With her newfound confidence and her new hard-won skills, Diya was able to move on with her life.

Surprisingly, one of the biggest indicators of success in global gender equality, and usually an overlooked measure, is an increase in the divorce rate. Having skills that provide regular cash that you have worked hard to earn, community, trust, and a general ability to see the world differently seems to have a similar effect the world over. When women are provided these opportunities, they gain the agency and resources to make their own long-term life decisions. Sometimes, the decision to end an abusive or destructive marriage is the first step towards a happier and more fulfilling life. This was not a measure that our social impact measurement bean counters in their corporate offices were focused on! But it became a valuable measure for us as we looked to effectively and deeply change individuals' lives.

While Diya's divorce and moving away was not good for the traditional impact measurement of employee retention, and frustrating for us in that we had to hire a less experienced tailor to replace her, (who, per our gender inclusion policy, had to be a woman), we were so happy for her newfound freedom and happiness. We were honoured to have been able to play a small role personally, and proud that Visible had played a highly influential role in this pivotal moment in Diya's life. Our joy at having one of our most dedicated workers in whom we had invested time, money and effort into training, abruptly leave because her divorce had finally come through was too complex to try to explain in our monthly customer newsletter! However it was the logical, positive consequence of following a fair trade model and of building a DNA of fairness across the organisation.

Control and Freedom: Cash is King (or Queen)

The belief that 'cash is king' was regularly reinforced by the team, and when we offered to develop various other benefit programs or structures that involved a monetary aspect, it would always come back to what was most important and what mattered most to them: cash in their pockets. Savings account? No, thanks. Pensions? No. Healthcare fund? No. Cash, cash, cash.

We managed the pot of money for the team as effectively as we could with multiple salary reviews, reflective of living wage market rates as well as comparisons with others within the company. We could have done more with pensions and other savings matches, but as we listened to what the team actually wanted, rather than imposing what we thought was best, we heard time and time again that cash in hand was always viewed as best. For them, in many ways cash was more dignifying than any of the other benefits. Being trapped in poverty with a lack of disposable income takes away personal freedom. And when freedom is taken away, so is dignity. When a person has disposable income, having choices and the dignity to be able to be in control of life decisions, the impact is massive. Eventually, we did provide multiple other benefits to the team - child care, school matching fees, healthcare fund and so on - which were appreciated by the team and by professional impact measurement assessors. Yet, after listening and adjusting to what the team told us, it was clear that none of these benefits were as impactful as cash.

Perhaps one of the biggest and least measured areas of the impact of having regular cash was the 'headspace' that those of us in privilege often take for granted. Having money that isn't being used for immediate survival needs gives you the ability to think and plan ahead. Some of the outcomes of this could be seen in a very clear and tangible way, but this massive impact was more often highly subjective and longer term. Perhaps it would be measurable further down the line as different decisions bore fruit.

Dignity: The Paradox of Upskilling

In addition to the measurable impact of cash, we also looked to expand impact across the company in ways that were more subjective. As mentioned before, employee retention rates were something that we were regularly advised to track and publicise as an indicator of success. We understood the basic premise behind the advice; a 'good' company would be somewhere people wanted to stay, while a 'bad' company was one where there would be a lot of staff turnover as disgruntled employees left. For us, this presented a paradox. We wanted employees to stay with us because we were a good company that treated employees well. But we also wanted employees to see such improvement in their skills that they felt more powerful than they had previously. Upskilling would give them the confidence to step into new positions and make them want to explore opportunities to utilise their newly acquired skills. One of the consequences of training and upskilling was that employees would want to go and work elsewhere if a growth opportunity presented itself. Even though it could reduce retention, we remained committed to providing training and opportunities for the team to gain skills to improve their lives. Their well being and success were, after all, a large part of our motivation for starting the business in the first place.

As staff members took the opportunities we offered to learn and grow, they began asking for a greater diversity of work that would further expand their skills. When we were presented with opportunities to work with higher-end designers and brands, we saw a win-win-win scenario. While this kind of work offered an overall lower percentage margin for us as a company, it presented a great net profit per hour of production. We proactively tried to find partners that wanted work done that was within our team's capability, but that would also stretch them. Products that they hadn't made before that required new techniques were fantastic opportunities to stretch and learn. Working with outside companies and designers also allowed us to focus on production quality rather than on marketing and redesigns.

As we undertook regular satisfaction reviews, it was great to see and hear that team members' job satisfaction sharply increased as they had increased opportunities to expand and stretch their skills. Not only was it the skills that they had acquired, but it was also the sense of greater control and a feeling of more dignity that they were experiencing. This impact was again hard to measure, but precious and what we were all about. Dignity was so impactful and yet so hard to measure.

We had both spent our careers striving to have more control over our lives and work paths. While financial success and security were not a big motivator for us compared to many of our peers, we both had enough experiences of having to deal with the consequences of other people's poor decisions that we craved more autonomy. We both relished the responsibility that came with autonomy, and we were aware of how incredibly fortunate we were to be able to pursue opportunities to gain more control in our work. In a large part, the freedom to pursue autonomy was the consequence of being born as a white male into a situation of economic privilege. We were born into the minority that had great power and privilege at this time in history. In part, our yearning for autonomy was the result of how we'd been raised, our personalities, and our life journeys. Both of us had travelled extensively and had chosen to challenge ourselves with non-traditional career moves (like buying a fair trade factory in India!). Now, it was an important priority to find ways for employees to also enjoy autonomy and dignity. We strove to help them gain as much control over their lives and work as possible. Seeing what this meant to these individuals was profound.

Greater Job Satisfaction

When we launched our new line of dress ties with pockets, we were initially focused on how much customers would appreciate a pioneering idea. We had great fun developing various designs of ties and trying to come up with unique ways to present and market these ties for different customers. The boss tie with room for a credit card and a business card; the golfer's tie with pockets for a few golf tees; the musician's tie with pockets for guitar pics. The list went on and on as we developed an incredible list of ties with different pockets. While a great idea for marketing purposes, the real challenge came when we were trying to produce all these different styles and designs.

Learning how to make a new product that no-one on the team had direct experience of initially proved to be incredibly challenging. The intricacy that was required left no margin for error. The majority of our team had the skills to do the job and genuinely were keen to stretch themselves. However not all of them started out with the same level of confidence or competence. In order to maintain our core value of quality, we knew that we were going to have to invest substantial time and energy in developing a team approach so that everyone could play to their strengths. After the initial buzz created with the product launch and kickstarter campaign, we decided to take over the whole factory for a few days and focus 100% on tie production. The first morning was incredibly frustrating with minimal progress being made and stress levels rising across the team. We decided to turn things upside down and focus on fun, fun, fun. We launched... 'The Tie Olympics'.

Starting with a simple challenge to complete a single tie order, we gradually increased the challenges, creating more obstacles. We ended up having various relays and incredibly arbitrary judging, especially from the East German judge! For the remainder of the next two days we created a number of semi-realistic scenarios with the goal of developing greater teamwork, expanding skill sets and increasingly productive. An urgent order suddenly came in from UK business man requesting five different styles to be made and shipped within a few hours. A few minutes later, we had an order from an Australian wedding organiser that wanted 5 different designs for each member of the wedding party. 30 minutes later a company in New Zealand placed an order for 10 ties to be given as gifts for their team's Christmas party.

As we juggled with the stress of situations later in our journey, we constantly looked back to how we had performed at the 'Tie Olympics', focusing on each others strength and finding ways to support each other to ensure that we were delivering a quality product. It was great to look back and remind ourselves of how far we had come as a team. It was a great way to address and live into our core value of fun. Fascinatingly, the greatest impact on the launch of this new product was less about the customer having amazing, fun ties, but it was the fun and camaraderie that was experienced by the team.

Expanding Horizons

We welcomed a multitude of visitors to come and see the factory in action. It was part of being open and honest about our model: being visible. Overall, the team loved it when we were able to have outsiders come and spend time inside the company. They willingly and generously shared their lives and culture, inviting visitors into their homes.

Preparing meals together and sharing community was a great way to deepen connection and trust with visitors, as well as providing an amazing and authentic cultural experience. It wasn't the most efficient use of the factory employees' time for our monthly productivity goals, but the positive impact and connections made it worth the temporary reduction in productivity.

It was also in line with our core value of fun when hosting visitors, Andy and I were often too over scheduled and stressed, focused on working through the never ending to-do list, rather than sitting down and being present in the moment. In hindsight, for us personally, it might have been better to embrace more of the fun that other members of the team were able to have with the visitors. While it's hard to definitively say how much of a factor these visits were in getting more orders, they definitely helped to build long-term loyalty and trust. Most significantly, they expanded the team's horizons.

Our team members genuinely looked forward to the visits, because they provided an opportunity to connect with people outside of their cultural sphere. Team members regularly told us that they dreamed of being able to work with more Westerners, to share their abilities and their passion for their culture, not just through work but through things such as food and dance. As they told us, the team loved being seen as whole people and not as people who had been unable to have an education, or people who could only be trusted with jobs that others perceived as menial. They wanted to be seen as people blessed with skills, who had worked hard to refine and develop those abilities.

Over the time running Visible Clothing, we had guests of at least 15 different nationalities visit the factory, and we shipped products to over 25 countries. As a relatively small social enterprise, we were grateful for the opportunity to work with many different designers from all over the world, meaning that staff were able to gain a wealth of experiences and massively expand their skill sets.

However, there were two sides to this coin. It was both laughable and somewhat frustrating when we would hear brands that we produced for, talking about "their team" or "their factory"; in their marketing materials! They were proudly championing the impact that "they were having on their team". Meanwhile we were the ones working like crazy with our team to keep our company on track and moving forward. It was frustrating to feel used by clients that we trusted, and to see others take credit for our work. Part of this was our egos and the fact that we had worked so hard to develop a culture that we wanted to be proud of. Part of it was business sense, in that we were trying to build the Visible brand, and for that we needed recognition of our successes. But the biggest part was our desire to protect the team and avoid exploitative poverty tourism. Welcoming often brash, sometimes overpowering, Westerners required a lot of trust when there was such a strong power dynamic in one direction, and so we tried to proactively prevent exploitation as much as possible.

While the work wasn't all about us, it meant a lot to us and we were proud of the work that the incredible team members were doing. In many ways, this isn't even our story to tell. It was the story of the team and their individual dignity.

Environmental Impact

As we mentioned, when we started out on our journey, environmental impact wasn't our primary focus. Galvanised as we were by the Rana Plaza tragedy, we were all about the people that were directly impacted. As we started to rebuild our wardrobes, we rapidly learnt how important and consequential the environmental impact of clothing manufacturing was, and the deep need for regeneration. Regenerative environmental impact has to be at the core of any business that wants to bring about long-term positive social change in the clothing industry.

Before we acquired the factory, our plans for environmental impact were primarily focused on having a systematic, environmentally minded approach to fabric procurement and fabric management. We spent a lot of time connecting with others in the ecosystem to learn more about certification, organics and environmentally responsible fabric sourcing. As owners of a factory, we wanted to use our platform to bring these learnings to our customers. We fondly remembered Johnald's experience of his first-time wearing bamboo undies, and the sheer joy and glee he had over his newly acquired, environmentally regenerative boxers! We wanted to experience that joy with our own products, and have others experience it too.

While we were skeptical about many of the sales pitches proposing the latest and greatest super-duper fabrics, we knew that sustainable fabrics were the way of the future. But after a long time reviewing and discussing samples, we were painfully aware of how little we still knew. Initially, we were impressed by how advanced some of our competitors were. And then we were equally unimpressed when we read the small print and saw that many of the new super-duper, world-changing fabrics were not as fabulous as they first appeared.

Frankly, for us, fabric sourcing was an incredible pain and something that we struggled with the entire time we ran Visible. There always seemed to be a million variables and challenges. From sourcing fabrics that could only be washed at a very specific temperature, to getting the exact colour dye that fit in the design specs, to getting the right kind of fibre blend that provided the most comfort and durability. Buying fabrics was a lot more challenging than we ever expected. We were left feeling like we were playing a game of Whack-a-Mole with one challenge popping up after the other and we were regularly unhappy with the end result.

We tried partnering with established organic suppliers. However, our model, in which we had a relatively large number of products, styles and colourways available, meant that we were not able to buy fabrics in massive volume and meet the high minimum order threshold. Additionally, while our customers talked about their desire to buy organic cotton, they weren't prepared to pay the premium that was required for organics. We weren't in the same position as some of our competitors who had sufficient demand and volumes to absorb the cost differences and therefore go 100% organic. So, we struggled to add organics in a truly meaningful way. After too much time trying and failing to buy ethically sourced organic fabrics in the tiny volumes that we could afford, we experimented with other approaches. We tried launching a collection focused on customised organic fabrics, thus entering into one of our biggest mistakes and steepest learning curves of the whole journey. It was a lengthy process with the procurement of these fabrics taking months. After extensive delays, we were left with contractual legal wrangling, along with the moral challenge of being asked to pay for fabrics that due to the delays, our buyers no longer wanted. Managing the squeeze along the supply chain from both sides was excruciating. It was a nightmare for a company that was trying to be real about the waste challenges in the sector.

Additionally, deepening connections with individual sellers at the local markets was great, because it allowed us to buy small amounts of other companies' leftover fabrics, but this too was an ethical minefield. On one occasion, we were super excited to have found a large amount of off-cut fabrics. They were fashion forward, unique, distinctive, appropriate to be utilised in a variety of different products and available at a great price. After completing the designing and sampling process, we were excited to go to market. You can imagine our horror when we saw those exact same distinctive fabrics being a major part of the new collection of a well known high street brand. We had unintentionally brought someone else's proprietary fabrics! Trying to get fabrics that weren't knockoffs or weren't from someone else's proprietary production runs, reduced our options.

It was also a difficult and often thankless challenge to maintain authentic story-telling with fabrics that we couldn't control directly. Any time we stated a claim about fabrics, be it that they were organic or anti-human-trafficking or anti-waste, or shared an environmental idea that we were working on, we were asked a multitude of questions from our customers that made us feel like we had to defend and justify our position with third party data. While we wanted to be challenged and asked questions, this didn't lead to more sales. Instead it set us back. We will be challenging you later in the book to ask hard questions, but it's important that this is not just an academic exercise, but rather a conversation intended to lead to more meaningful change.

For example, when we partnered with an incredible group fighting human trafficking who were making beautiful, high quality fabrics, we were asked relentless questions about how we knew that we could trust their impact story and who was auditing them. It was so frustrating that we had to jump through unnecessary hoops to articulate what we knew to be true. Even though we had had multiple face-to-face meetings and had met with women impacted by this organisation's work, we still had to endlessly defend and justify the choice. The high standards and detailed answers expected from a fair trade group far exceeded those that would ever be asked for mainstream profit-driven companies.

We were questioned on the biodegradability of the ink used in the screen prints. We had to learn all about silk- worms being killed in production and had many conversations about whether silk could ever be ethically made. We were questioned about the role of plastics in the wider clothing sector. We did an extensive review of our hangtag policy to reduce our micro plastic outputs. Often, while these were understandable concerns, and generally came from a good starting place, it was hard not to get bogged down by the negativity and nit-picking. Fascinatingly, marketing the story of caring for the environment was a lot easier and avoided the more complex issues associated with stories of poverty and people's personal life stories. Focusing on the environment, was far easy to share stats and objective data. It was less loaded and complex than telling the story of someone coming out of extreme poverty. Measuring tonnes of waste not going to a landfill was more easily digestible for a consumer, especially when compared to something like the incremental increase in dignity felt by an individual worker.

When we felt overwhelmed with the enormous challenge of fabric sourcing, we went back once again to the mantra of controlling what we could control. We went back to our core mission, and redoubled our efforts to make everything at the factory visible, including our environmental impact. After some false starts, and a lot of reflection, we chose to focus our efforts in this area on our in-house production and specifically on waste management. We decided to implement and focus on a zero waste production model.

Zero Waste Production

After 18 months of owning the business, our frustrating relationship with our landlord had sunk from being a recurring annoyance to a new low, requiring us to review our lease and legal options. We needed to find a better location where our team could have a better chance to flourish. We also wanted to have the factory layout and line production set up in a way that would allow for zero waste production. When the opportunity arose to relocate the factory, we decided it was time to make the changes we had been talking and dreaming about.

In the process of moving locations, we undertook our quarterly review of the inventory fabrics, specifically focusing on those that hadn't been touched in the last year. With our new zero waste lens, we were shocked to be reminded how many 'toxic' fabrics we had. Tens of thousands of pounds/dollars had been invested into these fabrics - both our own money and that of our investors. Some of this was our own fault, in that we had been overly ambitious in trusting feedback from sampling, giving us a false confidence that new collections would be successful with customers. Some of it was from our initial naivety, believing that all promises for purchase orders meant they were going to land, which they did not. But the biggest issue was simply the nature of our production model. We had a high number of options (product SKUs), which meant that a large amount of fabrics always had to be on hand, but were not always used. We repurposed and redesigned as much as possible, but were inevitably left with a lot of good quality leftover fabrics.

We had been impressed by some environmentally pioneering groups, both companies and non-profits in various sectors, with zero waste approaches. We admired the quality of their products as well as the authenticity of their impact stories. We had stopped using single-use plastics at the factory when we first took it over, but we needed to get more comprehensive about waste management. When we had bought our personal wardrobes, primarily online, we were blown away by the amount of packaging waste. The reliance of the ethical clothing industry on single-use plastic was shocking. For a sector that was focused on the greater good, there was an awful lot of environmental waste being created. While lots of clothing companies applauded themselves for sending packaging that were made from recycled materials, we, the customers, were left with bags of non- recyclable waste that we had to send to the landfill. We understood that there were some factors outside of our control as a company, such as the sticky plastic based address labels, but we believed there had to be a better way of managing the majority of our packaging.

When we sent out our first production run of t-shirts, we intentionally used compostable packaging. We weren't expecting all of our customers to suddenly become at-home composters (however great that might have been!) but we felt a moral obligation about our packaging, so we wanted to send the t-shirts out with end-of-life packaging in mind. It was an easy starting point that we could control.

Now, as factory owners, we completed a much deeper review and evaluation process. We ended up creating our own in-house packaging, designing a simple reusable tote bag with a reversible waterproof pocket into which the rest of the products could fit when packaged up. It wasn't high end, but had a great life cycle ahead after it had been used for packaging! Sometimes the delivery companies refused to use our packaging, as they had to transport everything in their pre-set single use boxes or containers. Where possible, however, we chose to ship with companies that were prepared to use our packaging. Our reversible bags cost us slightly more to produce than single use plastic bags, but they became a great marketing asset. The reversible bags were perhaps one of our simplest, values-aligned and fun innovations.

As we worked our way through the left-over fabrics that we used to make the packaging bags, we became more directly aware of the incredible amount of fabrics being wasted every day through offcuts. According to various reports, up to 25% of the fabrics that are typically brought into an apparel factory, exit the factory to go to the landfill. Patterns are aligned with fabrics and obviously the primary focus is on the design, and so fabrics need to be cut in specific ways, typically with a laser focus on the end look. Therefore, the amount of waste of offcuts from the design process alone is outrageous, before we even get into the waste created from production failings at the factory. Our waste percentage was substantially lower, but it was still considerable, approximately 10%, and so we wanted to make some changes.

We decided to start using all the fabric waste that we were producing. This dovetailed nicely with our need to find a more efficient way of packaging our products. The simple tote bags with the reversible waterproof pockets that were being made from left-overs were now being made from scraps.

In addition to the environmental impact, we were delighted to see that this environmentally conscious approach had a positive impact on personnel. Through this pivot to our business model, we were able to deploy some of the newer, less experienced tailors to make simpler products that required less finesse. Making our zero waste products was a great opportunity for them to practise and improve their skills. 'Waste' and 'mistakes' were now a selling point rather than a pain point. Rather than creating rejects which would end up in a landfill, off cut fabric waste was used to make cheaper but still sellable items. We also embraced new designers who came up with other creative ways to utilise fabric waste. Over the next year we tweaked and adjusted our zero-waste initiative, ultimately developing an eight-stage process:

1. Design - Our initial designs were adjusted to ensure that we were using every inch of fabric. Complementary accessories, headbands, scarves etc, were incorporated everywhere we possibly could, so that waste was minimised right from the outset.

2. Fabric purchasing – We continued to adjust our fabric sourcing strategy, being mindful of both the beginning and end of life usage of fabrics. Having learned some painful lessons already, we were able to drastically change the fabrics that came into the factory. New fabrics that we purchased had to work with our zero waste philosophy.

3. Local Shop – The area where the factory was based had a number of tourists passing through, so we invested heavily in an existing project: a local shop selling our products that, though still good quality, had been rejected for various reasons. Customers were able to try on and buy one-off products that were visibly (transparently) sold 'as is'. This outlet provided us with an opportunity to generate revenue from our rejects of samples and returns.

4. Launch of ongoing zero waste collection – Our design team got creative, from using cuffs on men's shirts that were intentionally set up to match with dresses for their daughters; to designs using multiple fabrics (offcuts) in one outfit; to contrasting fabrics that were used to create colourful boxer shorts - our popular 'Junk for your Junk' collection. We welcomed new ideas on how to be creative with scrap fabrics, and encouraged our wholesale customers to incorporate zero waste approaches into their sales process with promotional products that we made out of offcuts.

5. Scrunchies galore – Perhaps the biggest success of all was an unexpected comeback from the '80s. Our scrunchies were not only incredibly popular, especially when they complemented the main outfit, but were also a fantastic product to use for training some of our less experienced tailors.

6. The 'Rug Ladies' – We learned that longer scraps could be woven into beautiful rugs. We partnered with a local group of ladies who for various reasons, were only able to work from home. They were a wonderful women's collective and a compassionate community who affectionately referred to themselves as the 'Rug Ladies'. Their fun and casual style rugs weren't intended to compete with high end Persian rugs, but in addition to actually looking and feeling good, their rugs

presented a great talking point with customers about waste management.

7. Paper makers – At the end of the production process, however efficient and environmentally conscious it was, we were still left with a lot of scraps. For this waste, we identified and partnered with a local group of Tibetan refugees that made paper from fabric scraps and threads. We were impressed by the quality of their production, and so we looked for more ways to collaborate with them. Over time, we developed new designs together, including beautiful notebooks and gift accessory boxes made from scraps that complemented the clothing.

8. Packaging – We started using that same group's handmade paper in various packaging options. And, after the initial success of our reversible bags, we started making more creative bag designs and packaging with various waste fabrics.

It was a success for us that we were able to save huge amounts of our waste fabrics from being burnt or going to a landfill. But the bigger win was the tens of thousands of people in our network who were educated about the very serious issue of waste in the clothing sector. It gave our customers an opportunity to do something positive and act out their values regarding the environment. It gave our employees the chance to try new things and to be part of the solution. Our approach to zero waste had similarities to when we gave away all our clothes. Our direct impact, while important, was never going to be massive, but there was a possibility of starting a conversation, influencing a larger group of people, and collectively, we could have a massive impact.

15

Visible #3 - Cost: Pivots benefit people and profits

Every day was an adventure as a social-entrepreneur. The only thing that we knew for sure when the day began was that we could never predict what it would bring by the end! We also knew that, rather than getting attached to our ideas, or sticking doggedly to the way we had been doing things, we had to constantly evaluate and be humble enough to admit when something wasn't working. We had to be courageous enough to make a hard pivot to the business plan when necessary, while always holding to what we were trying to achieve in our minds and hearts.

For us, pivots were sometimes painful, partly when they became necessary after things hadn't worked out the way we had hoped or expected. Pivots were also powerful. Each time we admitted that things weren't working optimally and made pivots, the business grew, and we grew as leaders and entrepreneurs. We regularly undertook SWOT (strengths, weaknesses, opportunities, threats) analysis in various forms to assess where the business was and where it was heading. Based on what we learned, we made some adjustments. Some things were tweaked and improved. Others needed to be completely dropped. Occasionally we made substantial pivots.

Interestingly, these pivots brought us back to the '4 Buts' that we had identified as barriers to buying ethically at the start of this journey. All four pivots came down to our third and final 'visible': costs. As we learnt more about real customer behaviour as opposed to our preconceptions and expectations we responded and adjusted.

Pivot #1 - Moving from Brick & Mortar Stores to Online

Our first major pivot related to our sales channel strategy and the need to find the right price point. As mentioned earlier, when we bought the factory, we also acquired an online brand, Eternal Creation based in Australia. We felt confident we could grow that brand, primarily by expanding sales into new geographical markets. We were excited to work on expanding the product range to increase both revenues and margins. There was a smaller, but (we believed) reliable and consistent income stream coming from wholesale customers. We were not particularly excited about the amount of margin that we would be forced to share with our wholesale customers, so we projected only incremental growth for this sales channel.

However, we were not prepared for the bottom to fall out of the wholesale sales channel so quickly over the first 18 months that we owned the company. We began to hear about boutique after boutique closing down, as online retailers brought about a drastic change to consumer behaviour. It was heartbreaking. Through no fault of their own, many local, community-based shops lost their customers to cheaper and more accessible options. These small town boutiques, some of which had been passed on from generation to generation were forced to close their doors. Unfortunately for us, these types of stores were the backbone of Eternal Creation's (and what was now Visible's) wholesale market.

The change to shopping habits away from small brick and mortar stores was but one manifestation of the changing approach to clothing in the world. Historically, customers went to these boutiques to acquire products of superior quality to those available at larger chain stores. And, the opportunity to tangibly touch and connect with a product was, to many customers, still far superior to buying online. An initial review of the customer base from the boutique buyers showed an ageing population that brought clothes with a very different mindset to their millennial children or grand-children. This drastically different approach to clothing was led by those who were now coming into their purchasing prime, Gen Xers, who had grown up with the culture of fast fashion, where price point typically trumped quality and everything else.

We could see that due to these changes in consumer behaviour with boutiques closing left and right, our original wholesale strat-egy was not going to work. And so we made our first major pivot: putting more emphasis on online, direct to consumer sales. We always had online sales as a big part of the sales strategy, but we realised it was going to have to become an even bigger percentage of our overall revenue generation.

The shift to primarily selling online to these customers posed some major challenges for us as a small social enterprise trying to bring in a generation of new customers. Chief among these was the unrealistic expectations of customers, who had grown used to deliveries happening within days. This was entirely incompatible with our made-to-order, bespoke model. We were sitting on a lot of fabrics, machines and people with incredible skills, but not a lot of finished products. Even when we were at our most efficient, it was hard to turn things around overnight like many Western customers were now expecting.

We had a big focus on quality and how that quality was conveyed and shared with other customers. Rather than investing in the declining boutique model where quality could be conveyed and shared by touch, we invested in finding more ways for quality to be conveyed online.

Pivot #2 - The Love Of The Bargain

The Eternal Creation brand was at the heart of the business that we had acquired, and we had projected that a large % of our initial annual sales revenue would come from that brand. We knew there was a loyal customer base and were confident that the customer acquisition cost would remain relatively low as we built on the platform that had been created. Understanding the customer basis was critical and we had to learn some hard lessons at the beginning of our ownership. We agreed that we would try a few different approaches early on, being mindful of the fact that there was an established customer base for Eternal Creation already. We also wanted to re-engage with customers that had purchased from the brand in the past, but not recently.

We had seen from colleagues in the social enterprise sector that, while much time is spent analysing the margins and reviewing the hypothetical worth of a product, the hard reality is that a product is only worth the price that someone is prepared to pay for it. It could be very disheartening to see that, while we valued a product at a certain price point and knew how much work, effort and costs had gone into creating that product, if customers weren't prepared to pay for it, then the conversation was academic and our personal feelings were irrelevant.

As we mentioned earlier in addressing the 4 Buts, logically, if workers are being paid fairly, then products are going to cost more. If a small brand or company is trying to compete with much more established businesses, then costs are typically higher before any economies of scale kick in. Additionally, while ethically minded customers are often prepared to pay more than the average consumer, there are obviously limits as to how much more they are prepared to pay.

We were adamant that if we wanted to disrupt the clothing industry, then one of the things that we really wanted to challenge was the reliance on sales and bargains. We envisioned providing quality, fairly made clothing to our customers, alongside a little education about fair trade practices. We were convinced that by so doing, we could ensure that the race to the price bottom would become less common than in mainstream shopping. How wrong we were! It was like trying to get a moth to not go towards the light. The words 'discount', 'bargain', or 'sale' would cause a trigger in the brain and kickstart a whole other rationale of thinking. Regardless of the conversations that we had just been having on fairness, and the direct correlation between how much was paid for an ethically made product and how much a worker would be paid, the consumer brain was wired to love a deal. It was a painful and hard lesson for us to learn.

Earlier in the book, we addressed the 'But' of price point being the biggest barrier for ethical customers. It was mind blowing to us that the desire to find a bargain was so alive and well in ethically minded customers being, as much or even more than for standard consumers. Ethical clothing consumers put my university OJ story to shame! It's kind of ironic, and perhaps speaks directly to the immorality of the 'bargain culture' that it is socially acceptable to use the phrase 'got a steal' when a spectacular discount is had. It speaks to the actuality of what has probably happened: someone has actually been robbed of fair compensation for their labour. Some of the most generous-minded customers that we personally knew were the ones that unashamedly wanted bargains the most.

One of our beliefs coming into the business was that, if we could make the value of the product visible, first by having consistent good quality, then customers would be prepared to pay for it. The feedback that we received was that the first production run of t-shirts was exceptional in its quality and price point. We thought that by having a visible breakdown of the cost, being clear about the impact, and guaranteeing consistent good quality and excellent customer service, then we would be able to educate our customer on the true cost of ethical fashion, and would only need to use sales and heavy discounts very occasionally to clear old inventory.

We tried different methods for increasing the margins on our products. We deliberately adjusted designs so that more bells and whistles were added, be it cute bows on the girls' dresses or classy details on the cuffs and collars of our men's shirts. However, we were met with negative feedback when we tried to pass on those increases in production costs to the consumers. When we surveyed our customer base (which we tried to do every six months) the feedback we received consistently said two paradoxical - perhaps even contradictory - things. First, overwhelmingly, the customers wanted to know that we were maintaining a fair-trade ethos and that the workers were being paid fairly. The second piece of feed-back was the customer requested that we offer more sales. They wanted quality, ethically made clothes but only at heavily dis-counted prices. We came to the troubling conclusion that while our customers bought from us primarily for ethical reasons many weren't prepared to pay for ethical production.

Unless expectations were set early on and the focus and appreci-ation was on quality rather than ethics or price point, it was really hard for customers to see the direct correlation between the fact that paying less for a product meant that the workforce would be paid less. We had a few promotions where we offered products at a 'pay what you want' price point. It was fascinating to see what transpired when we gave complete freedom to the customer to name their price. Unfortunately, we didn't really get enough data to make a proper analysis, and perhaps it was an unfair question to ask of a customer who was simply wanting to buy clothes with no desire to become a pricing expert for ethical clothing! Similarly, we had a few other promos where customers were allowed to choose from three price points. This did provide some interesting data. However well we told the story, to a large extent the person who has made the product remained faceless. Yet, the responses from our values driven customers were surprising. Even when we specifically stated that 100% of the sales price would go directly to the tailoring team who had made the product, the vast majority of customers still consistently chose the lowest price point.

The complete contradiction in the behaviour and attitude of many fair-trade customers was a reality that we reluctantly learned to accept. While still believing that we could educate more consumers, we knew that it was going to be a long and difficult journey to bring about changes in behaviour. Ultimately, we decided that if we wanted to launch new products that had a price point that was fair for everyone - customers, our team and ourselves as a company - then we would have to build out our own Visible Clothing brand that promoted different expectations. We pivoted away from our reliance on the more established Eternal Creation Brand that we had initially relied upon for stable income and launched our next collection of men's shirts with no sales or loss leaders. Instead, the emphasis was on quality, quality, and quality. Quality designs, quality production, including better quality control and fair treatment of the team members working on the shirts, along with quality customer experience. While sales of this new collection weren't through the roof, margins were much higher and we began to feel more confident that our work, and the products' worth was being valued by the consumer. But it was an uphill battle to overcome the customer's bargin buzz.

Pivot #3 - Bespoke Production for Emerging Brands

After much effort we came to the realisation that no amount of customization would allow us to compete at scale as long as we were solely reliant upon the customised online direct to customer ecosystem. As sales to brick and mortar stores had already fallen off, we saw that we would need other revenue streams in order to create a stable and sustainable business.

A breakthrough for us came when we started producing at scale for third parties that were very keen to use fair trade and who were willing and able to pay the premium that was needed for quality production in an ethical way. These buyers were keen to work with us to utilise the stories of our impact to share with their customers. Finding ways to deepen personal connection with customers was a critical part of building brand loyalty for these, and indeed for any customers.

Producing for our in-house brand, Eternal Creation, meant that we had a proven model of low minimum production quantities, which lent itself perfectly to working with emerging and new brands. The more research that we did, the more we learned how big the demand was in the market for small production runs of consistent, quality production. We thought that, while it was an initial intense investment of time, working with these brands would lead to a consistent revenue source. Additionally, by being in control of the factory, we were the ones who could decide who we were producing for each quarter or even each week and plug the gaps and produce for our in-house brands when needed.

Once we made the pivot to really focus on working with other brands, we were inundated with requests to partner. It was encouraging to connect and learn more about people's personal stories, different approaches, and the good work that was happening in many different parts of the world. On many occasions, potential partners told us we were the "fairest fair-trade" factory that they had ever seen (flattering to hear), but that they weren't prepared to pay the price point that we were asking (disappointing to hear). As we look back at the journey with the benefit of hindsight, we see many times where we overly compromised, relentlessly trying to get other brands to work with us. We offered loss leaders (under-priced products to get the ball rolling) or worked at cost with no profit for us, but too often to no avail for long term success.

Yet sometimes, we were still amazed at the 'purity' of some in the sector. Many of the questions that we were asked were literally impossible to answer and took us way beyond the regular conversations and debates about the different types of fair trade certification. They seemed so detached from the reality of 21st century integrated supply chains. There were expectations on levels of accountability and transparency that were simply impossible to achieve. It reminded us of the conversations that we had early on with our initial crowdfunding campaign.

We wanted to establish trust relationships with these new brands and emerging designers. After all, they were going to be spending a lot of time at our factory and it wasn't going to be in anyone's interests for us to have to babysit them through the whole process. But, as we developed more trust and barriers started to get broken down, we were shocked by how much education was needed for these groups to even get started. While we admired their confidence and swagger and saw the value of their 'fake it til you make it' philosophy of starting a business, it presented a number of challenges when trying to actually plan and make projections. We weren't prepared for the amount of time that we had to spend educating start-up entrepreneurs who looked like they had it all together on paper, and yet were uneducated and underprepared behind the scenes.

Fortunately I had had enough experience of working with Andy and his wildly unrealistic targets and idealistic goals, so I knew how to evaluate what I was being told, and connect it with reality! It was critical to bring positivity to the process and to work together to agree on realistic numbers and goals rather than to be dismissive or condescending, even when a buyer's projections were absurdly unrealistic. We had sat in on enough meetings where a know-it-all had completely taken the air out of an entrepreneur's sails, simply by being negative and a 'wise guy' (and yes, it was always a guy). We made a policy of never saying or acting with an "I told you so" attitude. Instead, we baked in regular reviews and feedback loops so that we could get more and more aligned with partners as we tried to develop relationships for the long term.

It was critical to understand the motivations of those who we were working with in the sector. We had a number of partnerships that started off really great and, even after the initial excitement had faded (as it invariably did), were still based on great ideas, resulting in data to show that there was a good product-to-market fit. However, the reality of start-ups is that it takes a lot of time to get decent cash flow coming into the business, and often a lot longer to get to the point where there is profitability. We had both had extensive experience working with partners and volunteers, and we spent time tweaking and adjusting the process so that we could reduce our frustration. Patience is paramount. And too often, we were lacking it.

This was also shown by the lack of willingness to make sacrifices. Not only were we 'all in' on giving away all our clothes on the ethical clothing journey, but this journey had cost us both a lot financially, with massive opportunity costs. Visible Clothing was obviously our baby and we didn't expect others to be as committed to the project as we were. But, we did expect them to have some sort of understanding of our commitment to the mission and have empathy for that. Over time, we learnt once more to adjust our expectations, as well as our vetting process for partners.

Once the team had been trained to work with emerging designers, we reached out to our network to seek more purchase orders. Our secret sauce wasn't just the fact that our pattern master and tailors were able to consistently and efficiently make quality products, it was also that, generally speaking, we were responsive and direct communicators. We understood timelines and expectation-setting that many other small manufacturers did not. It took us a while, but we learned our lessons and over time owned our power.

In total we had sales conversations with over 150 different brands and start-ups, directly producing for more than 30 brands. As we got more and more repeat orders from brands that trusted us, including some that trusted us enough that they left us to process their orders from purchase to delivery, our confidence, in ourselves and in this sales strategy, continued to grow.

Pivot #4 - If Customers *HAD* To Buy Ethical, They Could Afford to

It took us a while, but the golden opportunity - that we discovered later than we wanted - took us all the way back to the start of our journey. Again, it was all about customer's motivation and values alignment.

By this point, we had come to understand the motivations of people who claimed they wanted to buy in line with their values. There was a spectrum of people in the ethical clothing marketing space, ranging from people dipping a toe in the waters of ethical fashion, to hardcore customers who would only buy from ethical clothing brands that met their standards. We got that. We came to realise that if customers had to buy ethical clothing (because they had made the choice to buy exclusively ethical clothing), then their decision making process was a lot clearer and logical, and the three other Buts were easier to overcome. This had been the case for us as we'd worked through our own processes of rebuilding our wardrobes. After our initial commitment, we HAD to buy in line with our values. We now realised that the same dynamic could apply for other customers too.

We identified a number of other groups that were driven by their values, making the logical conclusion that if they were going to be consistent with their values, they HAD to buy ethically. Once we had this realisation, we reached out to ethically minded businesses and organisations, and sampled a variety of clothing products that they could use to represent their values. School uniforms for values-driven schools, t-shirts and other merch for values-driven faith communities, kitchen aprons and chef's jackets for vegan restaurants; and crew uniforms for environmentally friendly shipping companies all came into the sampling process. Partnering with like minded, values-aligned institutions and businesses was the name of the game for us.

Additionally, in working with such groups, we felt a deep alignment not just with our core values but also with what we had been learning all along the journey. We weren't trying to push or sell products or convince people to buy more than they needed. Finding groups that had to buy, for example, uniforms, addressed that issue before it become a moral conundrum.

Lastly, and not really a pivot, but very much related to costs was our aggressive sales targets. Adding a mass volume play had long been a goal for the company. A major challenge for us was finding a good product-to-market fit at a price point that could work at scale. A couple of years into the business, we were still trying to crack this nut, but knew that it was imperative in order to generate more sizable revenues. We were cautious, because we had heard multiple stories of fair trade companies that thought they had hit the jackpot of breaking into the mainstream clothing sector, only to underestimate the challenges of working with massive corporations. It was disheartening to learn about good ideas not being given a chance due to a corporation chasing the immediate financial return, heedless of the longer-term consequences. Additionally, we had met entrepreneurs who had entered into tight legal contracts with corporations, only to find their good will and desire to share being exploited through poverty tourism and sensationalised and insensitive portrayals of the workers' lives.

Thankfully, as we entered into potential new partnerships, we were reminded of the greatness of humanity. When the myths of fast fashion were overcome, we were able to enter into genuine, empathetic partnerships with some serious players in the industry. These partners were looking for added value rather than extracted value and focused on finding ways for all the stakeholders to work together.

Bottom line: Pivots were the name of the game. Sometimes these pivots were intentional in trying to make more things visible and embracing the role in trying to show what was possible in the world of sustainability. And, sometimes pivots were necessary to adapt to changes in the industry and world. Through these major pivots, and many smaller tweaks and adjustments, we had improved the business model in a variety of ways over five years. We had at times been exhausted, but were often re-energised when we had a chance to reflect and appreciate all that was going on in the emerging ethical clothing sector. We were confident in our diverse revenue streams and had no shortage of ideas and improvements that we were ready to implement. We entered into 2020 ready to build on these established relationships. We were also excited about the new opportunities and success that we were sure the year would bring. We felt excited about an impactful year that lay ahead...

16

2020: The pandemic nightmare

But then...

In the early months of 2020, we had completed the final stages of the lengthy sampling process for a couple of large purchase orders that we had worked on for months. These were our largest purchase orders to date and both had great margins. These orders would secure a full year's worth of work for our team and we were actively exploring more partnerships. Additionally, we could see multiple additional doors opening for us as a direct result of these orders and had the machines and physical space to increase our in-house team as soon as we were ready. We were excited about doubling down on our zero waste approach and looking to increase our environmental sustainability initiatives. We had taken out some loans giving us the working capital that we needed to meet these large orders. We'd been asked to speak at several events and gatherings and were optimistic about continuing to raise awareness and promote the business in the wider sector. We were continuing to produce for many new and emerging brands, with a number of finished products just waiting for the final step in production before being able to be shipped. We were mid-way through the sample process with others, and bringing more potential purchase orders into the conversation every week. There was a lot in the pipeline.

On March 4th 2020, I was at an event promoting Visible with one of our larger clients, having a great conversation about the efficiency of our just-in-time production model. We were discussing the positive impact on production waste when not sitting on piles of unwanted inventory. It was encouraging and powerful to hear from an expert in the manufacturing sector that our model made sense to him. It felt that all the hard work and costs, reflections, pains, and pivots were finally paying off. Little did I know, this was going to be the last positive and encouraging conversation that I would have for many, many months.

Covid.

When the first government lockdown was mandated in India, we were told it was just for two weeks. It was unclear exactly what was going to happen after two weeks with an exponentially spreading disease. No government decision maker, scientific expert or even armchair expert had lived through such a thing before and predictions were differing wildly. However, what was most worrying for us was the confusion. We could only see an unstoppable disaster coming over the horizon. We were telling everyone we knew that this was going to last a lot longer than two weeks, but apart from being mentally prepared, we felt absolutely helpless.

Once again, we returned to our core values as we sought to make immediate decisions. India was slower to shut down than other places so we checked in with the team, mandated frequent handwashing, and encouraged the constant wearing of the masks that most of the team were already wearing. Before social distancing became a thing, we were encouraging it, although it was clear that it was a near impossible task in population-dense India.

While India took their time to shut down compared to other countries, once the India government mandated their first lockdown, it was an extreme one. The travel restrictions and factory shutdown rules were incredibly oppressive. The result was the creation of utter chaos. Fear and panic set in for our colleagues. The disaster had come over the horizon and was coming straight towards us.

We had entered the year with a positive bank balance, but it was just barely positive, and our contingency fund had been used up with the sampling process, as we had worked tirelessly to land those large purchase orders. Like almost all small businesses, we were nowhere near ready to withstand the pandemic and economic distress that was about to hit us. We were totally unprepared for wave upon wave of shut-downs and the knock-on effects that they would have.

It is easy to reimagine the situation and downplay just how crazy and scary that whole process was. Everyone felt terrified. While many of our contemporaries complained about having their kids out of school and the challenges of having to work from their dining room table rather than their plush corner offices, our colleagues at the factory had a very different experience. They talked about the life-threatening fear for their family members' lives, the lack of oxygen in the overrun hospitals, the lack of food transportation and diminishing options for buying food. There was grave uncertainty for their immediate as well as long-term futures. The stark contrast in the two groups experience's was staggering and a clear representation of all that we were working against. Those who had choices vs those who did not.

The lockdowns were an understandable measure to prevent millions more deaths, but they came at an incredible cost for small businesses, and evaporated many social entrepreneurs' dreams literally overnight. While we tried to 'control what we could control', COVID affected our team members and their families directly outside of our control, and the catastrophic impact across our supply chain was impossible for us influence. We realised early on that our zero waste, just-in-time production model, which we had painstakingly developed and refined over five years, did not have the twelve month plus contingency that was needed to continue operations. We worked relentlessly to find an alternative, to tweak or indeed fundamentally change our business model and strategy in order for the business to survive. We had a glimmer of hope at the end of the first lockdown. At this stage, while we had already lost a lot of customer base with cancelled orders and requests for full refunds, we were hanging on to 80% of our purchase orders, including some of our bigger ones. But we were hanging on, by a thread, almost literally.

In hindsight, we see that this was fictional optimism rather than reality. A global pandemic wasn't going to be overcome after a brief lockdown. For the second shut down, the Indian government mandated that the factory would have to close once again. This ongoing shut downs started to hit us hard. Really hard. And, there were rumours that the plan would be to have multiple more shut downs.

The two large purchase orders that we were on the cusp of beginning large scale production for, and which we had worked so hard to secure, understandably vanished. With offices and schools on indefinite shut down, there was no need for business attire or school uniforms. These orders were gone.

However, while we all were struggling to cope with such an horrific situation there were positive moments. We were encouraged by the response of our customers when we communicated honestly with them about our situation. We asked our individual historical customers to continue to support us with 100% of their contributions going directly to our Indian colleagues. Their willingness to support us with their our own personal donations, meant that we were able to keep paying our workers full salary for the full ten weeks of that lockdown. We were determined to keep working, to hold on for dear life and make it through this storm.

We went back to our business plan and looked at what we could salvage. We worked our way through the sample database and chased up with all of the leads, scrambling to find any groups that we could produce for in this new remote world. We went back to our existing customers and historical products and tried to repurpose fabrics and designs as best we could. We looked to see how we could produce masks at massive scale. We even explored PPE production.

We reviewed our production model and explored different potential opportunities. More social distancing with various shift models, remote working models and distributed production. While masks, loungewear and zoom friendly 'business' tops were the new outfits of choice, unless you were one of the big players who could write the rules about getting your supply chain moving, traditional clothing purchasing and production had been turned on its head. The world was in a tailspin and we were caught in the middle of it, not knowing which way was up, and with no way out.

In many ways the pandemic, as it played out in India, was a microcosm of so much of the struggle that we had been trying to change over the years. According to the UN report, over 200 million people in India were pushed back into extreme poverty during the pandemic. Those who were already vulnerable suffered the most.

When I was 11 years old, I remember having a business conversation with an entrepreneur for what I believe may have been the very first time. He graciously shared with me about his roller coaster business journey. My biggest take away was him telling me that "if you're prepared to throw enough money and enough grit at a business, you can always be successful". While my understanding of that statement has become more nuanced over the years, and I've learned a lot of lessons about letting things go, the essence of it helped me on my entrepreneurial journey. I have often thought back to that conversation as a reminder and an encouragement to stay the course. If a business is worth fighting for, and if you're prepared to put in the time and the necessary resources, there will always be a light at the end of the tunnel. Always. But in this situation, for the first time ever, I couldn't see a light at the end of the tunnel. It was pitch black. All that we could see was just despairing darkness.

Along with the government enforcement restrictions, there was just too much to overcome. The panic. The confusion. The fear. Whichever direction we looked in, it was bad. Bad, bad, bad.

The role of migrant workers in India is still hard for us to fully fathom. The early response to the COVID crisis created such an atmosphere of panic and there was massive return migration as millions moved around the country. The impact on lives wasn't just in the millions but in the tens of millions, with each daily update seeming to contradict the news of the day before with a more devastating update. The confusion between national, state and local governments meant that we were utterly confused as to which team members and supply chain partners could travel, wanted to travel, or weren't allowed to travel. It was chaos.

Over the next few months of repeated lockdowns, the team that we had poured so much time and effort into, started to disintegrate as they took care of their wider families. They made adjustments to their lifestyles as they sought to survive the pandemic with a national healthcare system that was in complete disarray. We were devastated by the terrible behaviour of some people who we thought were partners and friends, but who took advantage of the situation to help themselves at the expense of the rest of the team. Deliberately sabotaging potential exits and intentionally hindering others. To our great sorrow, we didn't have the money or the power to overcome the chaos, oppressive rules, and economic instability created by the pandemic. And for the first time in our journey of running Visible Clothing, this was a problem that we were unable to alleviate in person as we ourselves weren't allowed to travel to India.

We were consistently asked by various members what they should do based on their personal circumstances. Some of our colleagues were called back to their ancestral villages to take care of their wider family's needs. Others were forced to make lifestyle changes that forced them to stop working. Others decided that this was the moment to re-evaluate their personal situation and move physical locations. Was that what was best for the team members? Would it really help them for us to make promises of long term work opportunities that we had no idea that we could keep while the reality of the future was so unknown? Did we want to coerce or try to entice people to go against what they felt was best for themselves and their families? Was that the lasting impact that we wanted to have?

We looked at a variety of options and worked relentlessly to find a solution for visible to survive in the long-term. We didn't want this ambitious dream to end in failure. It was unbearable to contemplate the possibility of letting the team down, after years of working together and building trust. We tried to sell the business to a few potential buyers and explored opportunities for mergers and acquisitions with other groups that were better positioned than us. We started off trying to sell the company well below market price and then ended up trying to just get pennies on the dollar. We even came to agreements a couple of times to have the whole business acquired. But the world was changing by the day. We explored a variety of potential pivots and business models adjustments. However, it all fell through. Eventually we ran out of options.

We were reluctantly forced to close down our operations on the ground in India. We sold what we could and apologised to our investors. We tried to help team members get new jobs. Meanwhile, we were left with feelings of despair and even stronger feelings of shame and failure.

While we all experienced some chaos at the beginning of the pandemic, for many the usual world order was relatively quickly restored. Thus, the status quo of 'business as usual' continued to impose its devastating impact on the poorest and most low skilled workers. The contrast between the powerful and the powerless became even more apparent. History will show not only the funny stories of people who had the time to learn how to bake bread or play the ukulele, but the billions of dollars that were fraudulently stolen at the expense of the poor and the most vulnerable. What a contrast.

The final video call with our team was emotional. Team members were in tears with a mixture of sadness about the team they were about to leave behind and fear about the future that lay ahead. Some were angry, as the opportunities that they and their families had relied on for years had now gone. As owners, we too had profound feelings of sadness about what we were leaving behind. However, neither of us came close to tears on that last day (they would come later). We were not going to be successful with this business and we were carrying the weight of feeling complete and utter failure. We were profoundly gutted and thoroughly exhausted.

As you can see from the amount of times reflection is mentioned in this book, we have reviewed and reflected intensively on what we learned and on what we could have done better. The cutting room floor of this book is even more full of reflections and could'ves, should'ves and would'ves that didn't make it into the book. We don't have it all figured out, but with the passing of time, most of what happened made sense. However this final phase of the journey is still unfathomable. With the passing of time, it still doesn't feel done, or really feel closed. The whole thing was just... heartbreaking.

17

Today: What about you and your values?

When we closed Visible Clothing, we were deeply saddened that we were unable to bring our vision of 'Treating team-members fairly, influencing the clothing sector' to its fullest potential. However, we were, and remain, so grateful for this once in a lifetime opportunity to learn, to connect with like-minded people all across the globe, and to educate others on the injustices in the clothing industry and the beautiful alternative provided by fair trade. Most of all, we feel extremely fortunate to have had the opportunity to design, build and to put into practice a values driven business.

We started this journey by asking questions and doing research. We sincerely contemplated why there was such a disconnect between who we claimed to be and what our behaviour in fact was. The values that we spoke about were not the values that we were living into. And, as we asked and reflected more, we realised that we were asking the wrong questions. We needed to turn many of the questions on their head.

Despite the extreme stress and countless shenanigans that we experienced running Visible, our core beliefs not only remain the same, but have strengthened and deepened. We deeply mourn the loss of the factory, as well as the feeling of optimism for our company that we felt at the beginning of 2020. We had great belief about how we were going to be able to impact individuals as well as influencing the wider sector. Sadly for us and our team, that was a dream that we weren't able to bring into reality in this form.

However, our vision continues in new ways. We're both still 'all in' on buying ethical clothing, and making every purchase in line with our values. While not spending as much time researching brands as we did ten years ago, we still love to see new and innovative values-driven companies. We're excited about the future and see more and opportunities for meaningful impact in the ethical clothing sector. We have seen an expansion of values-driven businesses in the COVID recovery world. Even though it was devastating for Visible, and so many other businesses like us, the flip side of the coin appears to be a great awakening that COVID induced. For many individuals, this season was a chance to reevaluate and reassess, to thoughtfully consider who they wanted to be in their next life chapter. For us personally, COVID was not only a defining moment for our company, but also a pivotal moment in our long term business journey.

Over the last few years, we have become involved in a number of incredible ventures that have fueled our excitement for the future of values-driven businesses. It's hard to overstate just how much of a learning experience it was, being the Founders of Visible, and we've been able to apply the lessons learned from the good and not-so-good rollercoaster of Visible to a variety of other initiatives that we have been privileged to work on.

For me, Andy Lower, I have taken lots of my learnings from the Visible experience to work with a number of other social entrepreneurs. As Founder and CEO of early-stage investment Fund ADAP (A Different Approach to Poverty) Capital LLC, we've developed a systematic approach to invest and support values-driven social-entrepreneurs who are eradicating extreme poverty.

For me, Andy Showell-Rogers, I have been on a mission to leverage technology to build a business case for sustainability in the fashion industry and beyond. I remain involved in the clothing sector, working as Chief Impact Officer at Common Objective (CO), supporting other ethical clothing suppliers around the world as well as sharing my experiences with values-driven CEOs.

But enough about us.

What about you?

How are you feeling after reading this book? Earlier in the book, we talked about the 'wannabe social-entrepreneurs', people who spent time around us trying to believe that, by their proximity to social-entrepreneurs, that they were social-entrepreneurs. They loved all of the rollercoaster ride that is the life of an social-entrepreneur but weren't prepared to take the risk and buckle up for the journey. It was a crushing disappointment when we lost the factory, having to say goodbye to our beloved team, to five years of relentlessly hard work, to our personal investment, as well as that of our investors. Yet, neither of us regret taking the chance. We feel so strongly about this issue, and are still so appalled by the injustice in the fashion industry, that the unacceptable choice for us would have been to take no action at all.

Our challenge to you as the reader is to ask yourself whether you are being a spectator with your social impact? Are you reading books and surrounding yourself with social impact, watching others, or are you actually stepping up and doing something to create social impact? Are you offering opinions from the comfort of your armchair on the sidelines, hoping that somehow your proximity to impact people will somehow rub off and make you an impact person? Or are you getting stuck in and getting things done on the issues you care about?

At the start of the book, we outlined that we weren't sharing the story of our journey to elicit feelings of guilt. We do hope you've been challenged, but more than being shamed, we hope that you are feeling inspired and motivated. While we'd love for more people to go all in on the ethical clothing journey, giving away their clothing, running ethical clothing businesses, or other creative ideas, we know that's not realistic or practical for multiple reasons.

However, we do think there are many ways to have a positive impact that are perhaps more realistic. But it will no longer be talking about me or us but about you. What choices do you want to make? Who do you want to be? How are you going to live into your values?

Our journey has been all about asking questions and not conforming the status quo as the default. These are simple and practical ways where everyone can take action to make a difference in their own individual way. Hopefully they can encourage you to think about your role as you reflect on the 'Seven Rs'

The 'Seven Rs':

#1 - Rethink - How does your wardrobe represent your values?

The clothing that you buy is a reflection of who you are. Clothing perhaps more than almost any other element in your lives is a clear representation of who you are. You are the only one in control of how you think and act on these issues. It's not about current societal norms, or what your peers currently do, or the historical way that your parents bought clothes. Ultimately, you - and only you - are answerable for your own decisions. What you wear shows others who you are and what you value.

One of the easiest ways to live into your social justice values is to simply just say 'No' to clothes that are made in a sweatshop. We haven't bought any non-ethically made clothes for over 10 years. By refusing to wear someone else's pain on your body (can't believe I actually wrote that, but it is arguably what we do when we wear non-ethical clothes), you can stand up for the human rights of garment workers, and wear your heart for justice on your sleeve, both figuratively and literally. We talked earlier about the questions that we were asking ourselves. While some parts of the '4 buts' had legitimacy, most of the questions that were being asked were the wrong questions to be asking. Rethinking requires us to ask the right questions.

We decide how we think and how we represent our values. We can decide to rethink. Sorry. Let me rephrase that: You. You decide how you think and how you represent your values. You can decide to rethink.

#2 - Reduce – Do you really need this in your wardrobe?

Andy and I often talked about the growth vs. degrowth moral conundrum inherent in our business model. The company was focused on selling more and increasing consumption. Yes, it was all about good quality and ethical practices, but our business was dependent on increasing sales figures. The more we sold, the more impact we could have on our workforce. We wanted customers to buy more. Meanwhile, we ourselves were still revelling in the freedom that we felt from having minimal wardrobes. It was such a contradictory feeling. We learned to live with it by focusing on expanding to new customers rather than concentrating on just selling more to the same repeat customers. That was our business approach, but what about our personal degrowth journey? What do you really need in your wardrobe?

Under no circumstances did I ever need the 51 shirts that I had at the start of this journey. Yet, ironically, at that time, I often thought it would have been nice to have had more! After giving all my clothes away, it was so liberating to travel – especially to the factory - with practically all the clothes I owned in one moderately sized suitcase. I felt psychologically free from the excess that society encourages in all of us.

How much do you actually need? How much can you personally reduce? How can you be part of the degrowth mindset?

#3 - Repair – Is there any way you can reuse your current wardrobe?

Before beginning this journey, I had no idea just how easy it was to repair a pair of shoes. Admittedly, I couldn't get anywhere near good enough to do it myself, so it's not super easy, but cobblers do still exist and, from our experiences, they are very very good at what they do. Seamstresses and tailors are some of the most skilled individuals I've ever met. Finding a local tailor capable of making adjustments or repairs so that I have a custom-fitted item of clothing has been a game changer for my current wardrobe.

If we were to think about reuse and repair options for all items of clothing, our whole approach to our wardrobe shopping would be different. Reusing clothes and proactively repairing clothes means that the initial 'investment' in quality will give a far greater return. Its linked to the degrowth and zero waste philosophies. If I can keep extending the life of my well-loved clothes, then I'll get a better bang for my buck. It has also encouraged me to continue to invest in quality clothing that is not only made well and fairly, but from materials that will last longer.

What pieces of clothing do you already have that you can repair? How would you invest differently in your purchases if you had a repair approach?

#4 - Regenerate – How can you reduce the environmental impacts of the life cycle of your wardrobe?

We've talked in this book about Visible's environmental practices in the production of clothes, and our role at the front end of making an outfit. However, when we assess the impact on the climate of our clothes, we also need to be mindful of the end of life environmental impact. As a last resort, recycling is an option, but it's important to be honest about the reality of recycling. We shouldn't abdicate responsibility based on well-funded, but often misleading, propaganda campaigns that overstate the truth of recycling. The reality is that minimal amounts of our current recycling actually goes back into the supply chain in a positive way. Recycling in its current practice is more often a problem rather than a part of the solution. Genuine recycling will hopefully become a greater part of the ethical clothing ecosystem, but at the moment, we need to be mindful of greenwashing and think about how we personally can regenerate outside of the current recycling set up.

Upcycling has moved forward an incredible amount since we started our journey. There are so many innovative and incredible business models! While the initial phase of our journey of giving away all our clothes had so many eye-opening moments, it would even more so now, a decade on. We might not be able to have a zero waste approach to ALL our personal clothes, but there are options that we can explore about what we do with the majority of the fabrics that we own when they reach the end of their life cycle. They are our fabrics, and just because we can dump them in the bin does not mean that we dump moral responsibility for them. Whether we choose to regenerate and reduce the environmental impact of our wardrobe is on us. They are 'our' clothes, and therefore, it is 'our' waste also.

Taking it a step further, renting from brands or becoming part of local clothing swaps are accessible options for most of us. Do you need to 'own' all the clothes that you wear, or can you embrace a whole different ecosystem? How can you regenerate the life-cycle of your wardrobe?

#5 - Revalue – How do you treat your investment in your clothing ecosystem?

My wife and I have co-opted into our vocabulary the phrase, "taking care of our fibres", as we try to extend the life-cycle of the clothes that we value. If we are investing heavily in clothing quality, doesn't it make sense to try to take care of that investment? Washing clothes wisely, drying clothes sensibly, and generally being thoughtful about how we manage our clothes can make a huge difference to their quality and life cycle.

Past generations taught us to care for the things that we value. Only recently have cheaper, non-durable, essentially disposable clothing and accessories become a mainstay of society. If we say that we value people in the supply chain, then we need to act in a way that reflects that and how we value the clothes that they create.

Can we take more care to value our clothes, both out of respect for the amount of cash that we have invested in them, but also because we respect the workers that made them? How can you revalue the clothes that you already own?

#6 – Review – Are you using your voice to review and share opinions?

We should be voicing concerns and sharing reviews with companies that have questionable ethics. Over our journey, we have questioned many sales clerks about their wider company values. Haranguing a random, lower-level employee of a multinational company is perhaps not the most effective way, but when there are opportunities to speak up and voice opinions about the challenges and oppression in the supply chain, we have to use it.

On the flip side, sharing positive reviews, rather than the 'constructive feedback' that armchair experts often like to type away, is not only good for social-enterprise leaders, but can be critical to bringing in new customers to emerging start-up brands. We encourage you to have a look and if possible, both buy from them and proactively share your opinions in reviews. It will take a few minutes of your time, but the impact is all part of the wider movement we can be a part of. Reviews carry weight when they are authentic, thought through, and add value.

There are multiple ways for you to have a voice in the sector. Sharing this book with a friend or donating an extra copy to a local library(!), using social media platforms to support brands that you like, or joining movements that your values are aligned with, are just a few. Think creatively about ways you can proactively make a difference and how you can use your voice.

How can you review purchases? Are you being proactive in sharing your values with others?

#7 – Responsibility – What is your responsibility for the abuse in your supply chain?

This last R is perhaps the most important. Are we prepared to own the responsibility that comes with owning clothes? Andy and I weren't directly responsible for the Rana Plaza disaster. Nor were you. BUT - within such an oppressive and vile clothing ecosystem, what responsibility do you and I as individuals have? Do you pass on the responsibility buck to someone else in the supply chain? Consumers can make a difference in the world. Now you've read this book, you can't blame ignorance or lack of knowledge. What actions are you prepared to take with that responsibility?

We talked about our feelings of shame and failure as we brought the Visible factory to a close. Those same feelings of shame and failure often stop others from making progress or even starting on the journey. We encourage you to think through what the barriers are that are stopping you from taking responsibility. Yes, there are lots of areas of greyness and ambiguity, and we've talked about the challenges on our journey. But, the bottom line is that buying ethically, buying in line with values - your values - works.

What do you feel your responsibility is within the global supply chain? What would it look like for you to live into your values more?

Epilogue

Forty-one people, including the Rana Plaza owner Sohel Rana, his staff and the management of the five garment factories inside the building, were eventually charged with murder in relation to the April 2013 disaster. The investigation found evidence that these forty-one people had forced workers to enter the building just before it collapsed, even though the workers feared doing so because they could see the cracks that had appeared in the wall. None of those charged were clothing brands and all of them were minimally impacted as they continued their production with other similar factories. We're pleased that there was an investigation and some people were justifiable charged with murder. However, there is still a long way to go before we get anywhere close to justice.

Acknowledgments

We are so appreciative for the many, tens, even hundreds, of family, friends and professional relationships that helped us on this visible journey. We did consider printing out the lengthy list of the thousands of individual customers from visible.clothing and eternalcreation.com who had brought our products over the years but decided it would be professionally inappropriate. However, no business can be built without the faithful support of clients who are prepared to part with cash and specifically for us, we're especially thankful for those who were prepared to support our crowdfunding campaigns. We appreciate you buying into our vision before products had even been produced and we're thankful for your loyalty over the journey. We are also appreciative to the thousands of social media 'followers' who consistently posted and commented on our various products and campaigns. We appreciate you all buying into the vision and being willing to support the team by living into your values.

We were fortunate to work and collaborate with so many amazing brands and companies over the years. Tragically, so many were also devastatingly impacted by covid. We are thankful to have worked with Common Objective (CO) throughout the process and the incredible brands that are part of the amazing network that they have created. Their list of brands is great starting point for anyone wanting to get more involved in the ethical clothing sector and we'd encourage you to have a look there as a starting point if you're interested in buying more ethically made clothes.

Regarding the writing of this book, critically we'd firstly like to thank our editor, Sarah Symons. Thank you. Not just for the countless hours spent sharing your wisdom by filtering through various iterations of this book, but for the encouragement, positivity and belief in this project. Your work in the social impact sector has been profound and the books that you have written and edited are a large part of this impact. We were fortunate to work with you. Its cliche, but profoundly true: we wouldn't have got it done without you.

We are so thankful for the team and colleagues at Visible, especially those who worked so hard to bring the vision of fairness closer to reality. We learned so much from working with such an amazing team on the ground in India. Special thanks go to Thimgan, Steph and Bridget for going above and beyond on a regular basis. We appreciated the wider Visible team who brought into the mission and who helped to make things happen, specifically to Martin, Kyle, Dan, Julie, Scott, Jill & Gordon. Thanks also to Michelle, Todd, & Elisabeth for so generously sharing your legal expertise with us over the years.

There are the many others who we have had the privilege to work with and the honour to learn from. Including: Ron & Marlys, Jim, Craig for having the courage and conviction to support crazy ideas early on. Tim & Lisa, Jon, Beth & Howard, Donald, Greg & Lorrie, Kevin, Mark, Barnaby & Ellen, for helping to refine and improve approaches to have a deeper impact.

There were those involved in the writing of this book, who both knowingly and unknowing had a profound impact on this process. Specific thanks to: John & Cathy, for your friendship, support and generosity of time, treasurer and talent; to Scott for following through on commitments and acting with a spine and heart (literally an almost new one!); to Linda & Simi for patiently helping to expand views on inclusivity; to Peggy for allowing such generous use of the Vaughan family cabin for numerous writing retreats; to Scott for listening and challenging to move from 1.0 to 2.0; to Allison for patiently helping to develop new ways of thinking on mindfulness and graciously addressing cognitive behaviours; to Sam for talking sense and keeping all the trains moving on time; to Robin, Joshana & Tina for using their black and red pens to help random thoughts become cohesive sentences; to Andrew for helping us to add up numbers; to Jonathan for being such a good friend; and to Brian & Liz for being honest and positive.

On a more personal level, we're thankful for the generosity of our families, Jane & Gordon and John & Elizabeth specifically for helping launch our crowdfunder and kickstarter campaigns.

Lastly, we already expressed our gratitude to our wives Jessica and Caroline at the start of this book, but it would be very remiss of us not to thank their incredible offspring, our kids, Marloe & Levi and Jack & Eli. Thanks for being on this journey with us; for learning patience as we took phone calls at all hours of day and night; for consciously and subconsciously challenging us and encouraging us to be the best version of ourselves; and for the many sacrifices you made as we disappeared on countless trips. We're so thankful and proud of you.

Appendix: List of reports

- http://www.telegraph.co.uk/news/worldnews/asia/
bangladesh/10041197/Bangladesh-building-collapse-Dhaka-
buildings-not-given-final-safety-clearance.html
- http://www.cleanclothes.org/news/2011/12/15/thats-it-
sportswear-fire-one-year-on-workers- still-dying-in-unsafe-
buildings
- http://www.cbc.ca/news/world/bangladesh-fire-
kills-112-at-wal-mart-supplier-1.1179644
- http://www.ibtimes.co.uk/bangladesh-arrests-owners-
smart-export-factory-deadly-429438
- http://www.cbc.ca/news/world/bangladesh-factory-
that-burned-had-locked-exit-worker-alleges-1.1315297
- http://www.cbc.ca/news/world/bangladesh-garment-
factory-fire-kills-at-least-10-people- 1.1930120
- http://cpd.org.bd/wp-content/uploads/2013/09/CPD-
on-Minimum-Wage.pdf
- http://www.reuters.com/article/2013/05/02/us-bangla-
desh-garments-special-report- idUSBRE9411CX20130502
- http://cpd.org.bd/wp-content/uploads/2013/09/CPD-
on-Minimum-Wage.pdf

- http://www.labourbehindthelabel.org/news/item/1179-new-research-shows-clothing-factory-workers-seriously-malnourished
- http://cpd.org.bd/wp-content/uploads/2013/09/CPD-on-Minimum-Wage.pdf
- http://betterfactories.org/?p=862
- http://www.bbc.co.uk/news/world-asia-24453165
- http://www.thestar.com/news/world/clothesonyour-back/2013/10/11/i_got_hired_at_a_bangladesh_sweat-shop_meet_my_9yearold_boss.html
- http://www.buzzfeed.com/sapna/meet-the-reporter-who-worked-undercover-in-a-bangladesh-clot#.rfbVOrr-NZq
- http://www.telegraph.co.uk/news/worldnews/asia/bangladesh/10783733/Bangladeshs-Rana-Plaza-tragedy-lives-on-for-the-child-workers-who-survived.html
- http://qz.com/404897/the-death-toll-from-a-footwear-factory-fire-in-the-philippines-has- risen-to-72/
- http://www.globallabourrights.org/alerts/rana-plaza-bangladesh-anniversary-a-look-back-and- forward
- http://www.ilo.org/global/about-the-ilo/newsroom/news/WCMS_221568/lang--en/index.html
- http://www.moneywise.co.uk/news/2009-09-17/are-your-clothes-covered
- http://www.goodhousekeeping.co.uk/money/the-cost-of-an-average-british-wardrobe
- http://www.cleanclothes.org
- Wages and working hours in the textiles, clothing, leather and footwear industries - International Labour Organisation Report, 2014
- Labor Rights Violations in Vietnam's Export Manufacturing Sector, Worker Rights Consortium May 2013 "Whoever

Raises their Head Suffers the Most" Workers' Rights in Bangladesh's Garment Factories

○ Global Dialogue Forum on Wages and Working Hours in the Textiles, Clothing, Leather and Footwear Industries – 2014

○ Work Faster or Get Out, HRW Report on Cambodia

○ Shop Til They Drop Report on Cambodia Malnutrition/ Faintings from Labour Behind the Label

○ Better Together Report (2013)

○ Experts by Experience: Workers Perspectives on Fainting in Factories

○ Wages and working hours in the textiles, clothing, leather and footwear industries -

○ International Labour Organisation Report, 2014

○ Better Work: Stage II Global Compliance Synthesis Report 2009–2012, International Labour

○ Office and International Finance Corportation (2013)

○ Wages and working hours in the textiles, clothing, leather and footwear industries -

○ International Labour Organisation Report, 2014

○ WRAP , Valuing Our Clothes, 2011

www.ingramcontent.com/pod-product-compliance
Lightning Source LLC
Chambersburg PA
CBHW060916120626
46553CB00001B/350